GOING OFF THE RAILS

Disaster Postcards From the Trackside
1900-1915

JOHN HANNAVY

First published in 2026 by
Whittles Publishing,
an imprint of Porto Press Ltd.
3 Connaught Road, St Albans, AL3 5RX

All rights reserved. No part of this publication may be reproduced, stored in a retrieval system, or transmitted in any form or by any means, electronic, mechanical, photocopying, recording or otherwise, without prior permission in writing from the publisher.
The author has made every effort to ensure the accuracy of information contained in this publication, but assume no responsibility for any errors, inaccuracies, inconsistencies and omissions. Likewise, every effort has been made to contact copyright holders. If any copyright material has been reproduced unwittingly and without permission the Publisher will gladly receive information enabling them to rectify any error or omission in subsequent editions.

Text, cover and page design copyright © 2026 John Hannavy

British Library Cataloguing in Publication Data
A CIP record for this book is available from the British Library

ISBN: 9781849957229

The rights of John Hannavy to be identified as the Author of this work has been asserted by him in accordance with the Copyright, Design and Patents Act 1988.

Printed and bound in Great Britain, using paper from responsible sources, by CPI Printing

To order please go to our website
www.whittlespublishing.com
or contact our distributor,
BookSource, 50 Cambuslang Road, Clydesmill Industrial Estate, Glasgow G32 8NB.
Telephone 0141 642 9192

Thanks to John Spear, Mark Fynn, and the owners of three private collections for permission to use some of their images in this book. The majority of the postcards are from the author's collection.

Cover images: The railway accident at Blairgowrie which occurred on 19 December 1906 is described fully in the text. Disaster postcards were only rarely printed in colour – a much more expensive process than monochrome. The inset shows another rare colour example, the recovery of the Glasgow & South Western Railway (G&SWR) 4-4-0 locomotive after a collision with a Caledonian Railway train outside Gretna Station in May 1901.

Title page: Working on the railways was, in many ways, more dangerous than travelling on them. This unusual photograph is one of a series taken in 1906 when a vehicle ran out of control down and into the stationmaster's house at St. Helens Junction in 1906. Opened in 1830 as a halt on the Liverpool and Manchester Railway (L&MR), St. Helens Junction is still in use today, now one of the oldest working railway stations in the world

Contents page: Saltcoats Station in Ayrshire, one of two stations in the seaside town, was operated by the G&SWR. This postcard shows the wreckage after 81 people were injured when a G&SWR passenger train ploughed into the back of another. A combination of human errors were recorded as the cause. The following abbreviations are used throughout this book:

CR	Caledonian Railway	L&YR	Lancashire & Yorkshire Railway
FR	Furness Railway	L&MR	Liverpool & Manchester Railway
G&SWR	Glasgow & South Western Railway	LB&SCR	London, Brighton & South Coast Railway
GCR	Great Central Railway	L&NWR	London & North Western Railway
GER	Great Eastern Railway	MR	Midland Railway
GNR	Great Northern Railway	NBR	North British Railway
GWR	Great Western Railway	NER	North Eastern Railway
HR	Highland Railway	SE&CR	South Eastern & Chatham Railway

CONTENTS

'THE DIVER' AND OTHER STORIES	5
1900 – A DISASTROUS START TO A NEW CENTURY	20
1901 – THE FIRST POSTCARDS OF RAILWAY ACCIDENTS	23
1902 – 'I FEARED IF I SAID ANYTHING, I WOULD CAUSE A PANIC'	25
1903 – 'OUR EPIDEMIC OF RAILWAY DISASTERS	29
1904 – 'A SINGULAR MISHAP'	34
1905 – PHOTOGRAPHERS WERE QUICKLY ON THE SCENE	39
1906 – AT LEAST THE WHISKY SURVIVED UNDAMAGED	51
1907 – PULLING THE WRONG LEVER	63
1908 – 'GOOD GOD! HE WILL BE IN TO THE COAL TRAIN!'	72
1909 – NOT A SUITABLE CLASS OF ENGINE...	75
1910 – 'WILL YOU KISS ME BEFORE I DIE'	78
1911 – 'GOOD GOD! THERE IS A MINERAL ON No.1'	89
1912 – 'THE DAMAGED BRIDGE BORE STRIKING TESTIMONY'	92
1913 – 'THERE WAS A BLOCK ON THE LINE AT COLCHESTER'	96
1914 – THE APRIL DAY THE 'FLYING SCOTSMAN' CAME OFF THE RAILS	100
1915 – QUINTINSHILL – THE RAILWAY'S DARKEST DAY	104
INDEX	112

SERIOUS RAILWAY SMASH AT SALTCOATS, OVER 80 INJURED. 18th AUGUST, 1906.

'THE DIVER' AND OTHER STORIES

When the 1829 Rainhill Trials on the Liverpool & Manchester Railway were re-enacted to mark the 150th anniversary of the occasion – which actually took place in 1980 – thankfully one notable moment from that day was not replicated.

The story of how, on the railway's inaugural day of operation, William Huskisson MP became the first person to be killed on Britain's railways has been told on many occasions – and is actually inaccurate – and how Robert Stephenson's pioneering steam engine *Rocket*, the most famous of all the early locomotives was the culprit.

While it is true that Huskisson was killed, struck by a train hauled by *Rocket* as he walked along the line at Parkside Station to greet the Duke of Wellington on whose train he had been travelling, two earlier fatalities had been reported in the railway's short history, both killed by goods trains.

opposite: A replica of Robert Stephenson's *Rocket*, taking part in the 'Rocket 150' re-enactment of the Rainhill Trials in May 1980.

below: Broughton Station – seen here in a postcard c.1907 – scene of the earliest known instance of someone being drunk in charge of a train. The station was originally opened by the Furness Railway (FR) in 1848. It initially served as the terminus of the Barrow to Kirkby-in Furness line and was opened to increase mineral traffic from nearby copper mines. The route was extended as far as Coniston in 1859. Passenger services were withdrawn in 1958, and goods trains four years later. The station building is now a private house.

below: On 9 August 1873, the *Illustrated London News,* reported that 13 died and 30 were injured in the crash at Wigan North Western Station on 3 August. First Class injured were taken to the First Class Waiting Room, lower orders to their respective waiting rooms, or treated on the platform. Sir John Anson, Baronet, was taken to the Royal Hotel where he later died.

Huskisson did not see *Rocket* bearing down on him on the other line. He thus became the first person to be killed by a passenger train.

The fact that this new mode of transport brought with it severe risks was not lost on either parliamentarians or the general public, and there would be lengthy debates, not just about the safety of steam trains, but about the effects of travelling at speed on the human body.

That event, of course, happened a few years before practical photography was first demonstrated, and decades before the medium would be able to record it effectively. While photography and the steam railways came along at about the same time, it would be many years before a moving train could be photographed. The new medium was still a very long way from being able to capture 'instantaneous' photographs, and

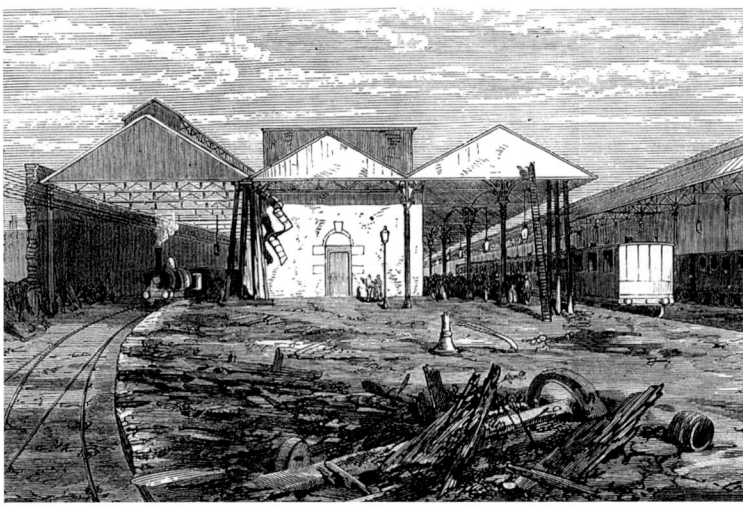

left: A missing section of track caused the Folkestone to London Boat Train derailment at Staplehurst on 9 June 1865. The workman waving a red warning flag was too close to allow the brakes to be applied. Ten died and 40 were injured. Charles Dickens escaped unhurt, and tended to the injured. His mistress, Ellen Lawless Ternan, and her mother, travelling with him on the train, were unhurt. In the novel *Our Mutual Friend*, he later wrote 'I remember with devout thankfulness that I can never be much nearer parting company with my readers for ever, than I was then, until there shall be written against my life, the two words with which I have this day closed this book, THE END.'

it would be left to illustrators to draw evocative scenes of the railway's many accidents.

By the dawn of the postcard era, taking photographs 'on location' was becoming much more straightforward with the advent of commercially available 'dry plates' replacing the need for photographers to coat their own.

Relatively early on, minimum construction standards were introduced in Britain, with a move towards safer standards of operation – but rules were not always observed.

In September 1876, probably for the first time in railway history, a Furness Railway Company driver and crew were effectively charged with being drunk in charge of a train. However, such an offence did not specifically exist on the statute books back then, so they were charged with being 'drunk while in the execution of their duty'.

The scene of the incident was the little station at Broughton-in-Furness, and the affair was reported in considerable detail in the local newspaper, the *Barrow Post*.

below: Dickens ministering to the injured, from the magazine *The Penny Illustrated Paper*.

'Henry Tyson, Station Master at Broughton, said that on Saturday at 11am, on the arrival of a ballast train from Coniston at his station, he found the three men under the influence of drink. The driver was insensibly drunk, and was lying on the footplate of his engine, the fireman being in charge of the engine,

Some accidents would have been worse had it not been for the actions of the crews. On 13 October 1872, with single line operation through a deep cutting near Winchburgh in West Lothian, two trains approached each other. Even with both crews' attempts to stop their trains, in time 17 died and 35 were injured in Scotland's first head on railway collision, including one of the drivers.

and was also under the influence of drink. The guard was in his van and was not sober.'

Tyson himself ran the train on to a siding and locked the points before telegraphing the Locomotive Foreman and contacting the police. Needless to say, all three crew pleaded guilty, the driver being imprisoned, the other two fined. The careers of all three had reached an abrupt end. The magistrate described the actions of Thomas Wilson, the driver, as 'a most serious evil'. Being drunk in charge of a heavily-laden railway train at any time would be considered appalling, but at 11am on a Saturday morning it was considered to be all the more reprehensible.

That this particular incident did not cause a serious accident was remarkable if, as the report said, the driver was 'insensibly drunk'. A bit of

In Abergele, North Wales, is a memorial to those who lost their lives in the railway disaster which took place on 20 August 1868. It was the worst railway disaster to have yet occurred in Great Britain. A brake-van and six wagons carrying cannisters of paraffin ran down a gradient into the path of the express from Holyhead and exploded, killing 33 people.

journalistic exaggeration may have been involved, as had he been totally incapable, he could never have brought the train to a halt in the station.

The brakes on early trains were inefficient, and a ballast train would have been difficult to stop even if the driver was sober – although the weight of the train and a slight incline as it approached the station would have worked in his favour. Had the incident been more serious, and taken place a few years later, doubtless local photographers would have been out with their large glass plate cameras to capture the moment for posterity.

When I first came across 'disaster' postcards in the late 1960s – those first were of an horrific mining disaster in Wigan, Lancashire – my immediate response was that anyone who collected such things must have a rather macabre streak in them, as these cards were often graphic in their depiction of serious and often fatal accidents.

But such a response falls in to the trap of believing that today's sensibilities and those of the Edwardians ought not to be the same – which they most certainly are – and that we are much less ghoulish and much more civilised. Not true, of course, as we watch footage of disasters on television which our predecessors would have baulked at and found truly horrific.

Not all fatal train crashes in the closing years of the 19th century were as a result of accidents, of course – some were as a result of weeks, if not months, of planning.

While in Victorian Britain and elsewhere, we simply read about disasters, in the USA entrepreneurs went much further and re-imagined the

below: First published in *The Graphic* on 10 September 1898, Leonard Brightwell's photograph of the aftermath of the crash on 2 September at Wellingborough fully captured the scale of the disaster. It was caused by a porter's trolley laden with mail fouling the tracks and derailing a Manchester-bound express. Some reports said the postman had lost control of the trolley which slipped down a slope on the platform. *The Graphic* initially suggested local boys had been the culprits, while later reporting that "Lieutenant Colonel Yorke, of the Board of Trade, opened an enquiry into the circumstances of the accident at Wellingborough on Monday, when the boys sought to show that they did not push the barrow on to the line, but that it ran off the platform of itself." Seven died and 65 were injured. The boys were not held culpable.

above: Three pictures from the staged collision at 'Crush', Texas. A press picture of the two trains the evening before.

above right: Just a second before the collision.

right: The crowds surge at Crush after the collision had taken place.

bottom: One of the attractions at the California State Fair in the early 1900s, was a staged head-on collision of two locomotives. Such shows ceased when the USA entered World War. By 1913, when this picture of two 'State Fair Specials' colliding was published, the collision was also filmed – photographers having set their cameras just 50 feet from the specially-laid track. The locomotives were each travelling at 45mph when they collided. In the movie, the driver of the left-hand locomotive can be seen jumping from his cab just six seconds before the collision.

train crash as specially-staged entertainment – for which, they discovered, the fascinated public were willing to travel considerable distances and pay for train tickets to see the spectacle. Such events offered good promotion for several American railway companies, and a lucrative additional income stream. But if things went wrong, the price to be paid could be considerable.

One such event was staged between Dallas and Houston in Texas in September 1896 where, on a specially-laid four-mile stretch of track, two redundant 32-ton Baldwin locomotives from the Missouri-Kansas-Texas

above: A series of cards published early in the postcard era by the Museum of Tsar Alexander III in St. Petersburg, re-used images of the 1888 derailment of the royal train at Borki near present-day Kharkiv in Ukraine. The over-weight double-headed train with 15 coaches was travelling at express speed on track designed for heavier, but much slower, freight trains. 23 people died in the accident.

left: The wreck of the Columbian' at Odessa Minnesota on just a week before Christmas 1911, occurred when the 'Columbian' running from Tacoma to Chicago was being held at signals. It was rear-ended by another train on the same track. Eight passengers and two railway employees were killed.

above: From a series of postcards published shortly after the accident in 1910, 0-6-0 locomotive No. 521 belonging to the Isthmian Canal Company is seen hanging off a partially-collapsed bridge at Miraflores during the construction of the Panama Canal. Five people died and seven were injured in the accident, one of many accidents during the construction of the canal.

right: The worst accident to occur on the New York City elevated railways, happened on the 9th Avenue 'L' on 11 September 1905 when 13 died and 48 suffered serious injuries. The train, travelling at speed, had been erroneously switched on to a tight curve leading to the 6th Avenue line, and hit the curve at about 30mph instead of the 9mph permissible maximum. Postcards of the wreckage were published widely.

Railroad, known, from its M-K-T initials, as 'Katy', and each hauling six ballast-filled boxcars, were driven towards each other at speed in front of an estimated 40,000 spectators – who had, of course, all travelled to the venue by train. The organisers had estimated that each train would be travelling at 35mph at the point of collision, but is was reported that they were going much faster than that. The idea had been suggested by

one of the 'Katy' employees, William Crush, as a promotional exercise to raise the railway's profile. A temporary town was set up, with shops, bars, a fairground and other entertainments, and the organiser called it 'Crush City'

Extensive advice was taken from experts in an effort to bring some sort of risk-management to bear on proceedings, and it was given the go-ahead as long as the public were kept 200 yards away from the track. Assurances were given by engineering experts and the manufacturers that the estimated combined speed of 70mph was within the safety tolerances

left and below: The May 1908 train crash at Contich (sometimes spelled 'Kontich') a few miles from Antwerp in Belgium, occurred when a points error diverted an express train into a bay platform where a passenger train full of pilgrims on their way to a local shrine was waiting to depart. Forty people – all of them on the waiting train – were killed, and over 100 injured. Postcards from several local publishers were quickly on sale.

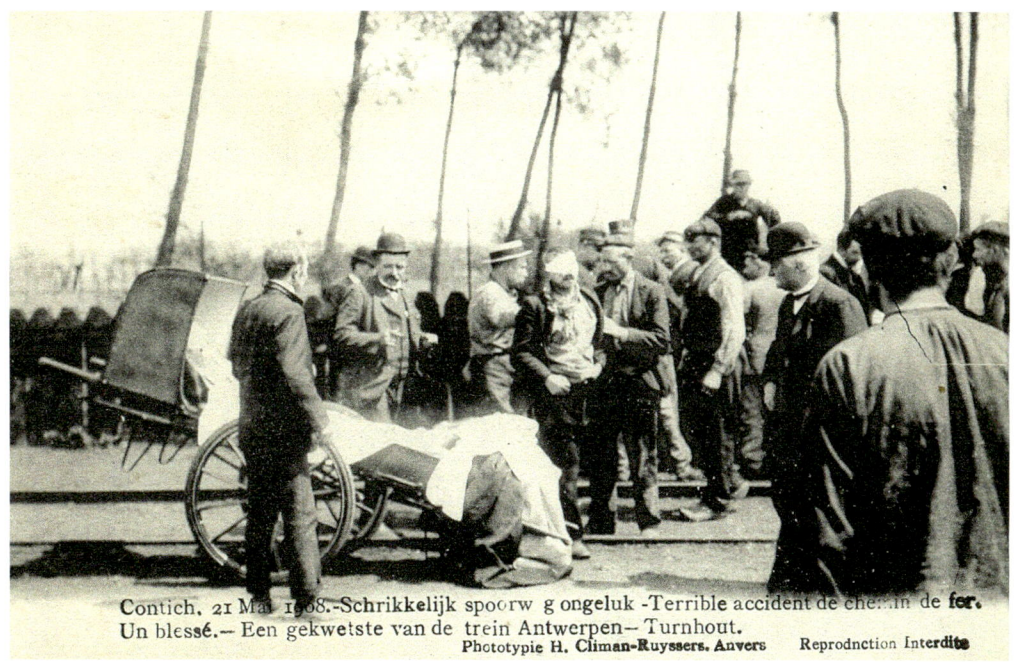

above and right: On 10 September 1910, at Bernay near Cherbourg on the Cotentin Peninsula in France, seven people died when a train, trying to make up lost. time and travelling well in excess of the maximum permitted speed, came off the tracks with devastating effect.

of the locomotives' boilers, and that the boilers would not explode – but they did. The photographer, Jarvis 'Joe' Deane was hit by a flying bolt and blinded in one eye, and two spectators were killed by flying debris. Luckily, Deane had already taken his pictures before he was injured.

The only real difference between then and now is that today's onlookers get their phones out and then circulate images on social media. The Victorians and Edwardians waited a couple of days and then bought and mailed pictures in exactly the same way.

Well into the early years of the 20th century, newspapers were either not photographically illustrated at all, or used photographs only very sparingly – reproducing them was an expensive proposition, and one which considerably lengthened the time needed to prepare any edition of the newspaper for the presses. Thus, many disasters were simply described in detailed texts, and were perhaps accompanied by a quickly executed line drawing or woodcut in order to get the stories into print quickly.

Limited edition runs of photographically-illustrated postcards, on the other hand, could be produced quickly and cheaply and, in effect, became

left: The driver was killed and the fireman injured in this derailment at Westerly, Rhode Island, in the USA, on 10 July 1911. Westerly Station is still operational today, but is unmanned. Despite being the subject of several postcards, the accident seems to have been under-reported when compared with the accident outside Bridgeport, Connecticut the following day, which killed 14 people.

below: The wreck of an American 0-8-0 locomotive, location unknown, c.1910.

right: An unusual postcard produced by Valentine of Dundee, showing the train crew on the ill-fated train which was on the Tay Bridge when it collapsed on 28 December 1879, together with the passengers' used ticket stubs retained at St. Fort Station. The card was produced in 1904 marking 25 years since the disaster.

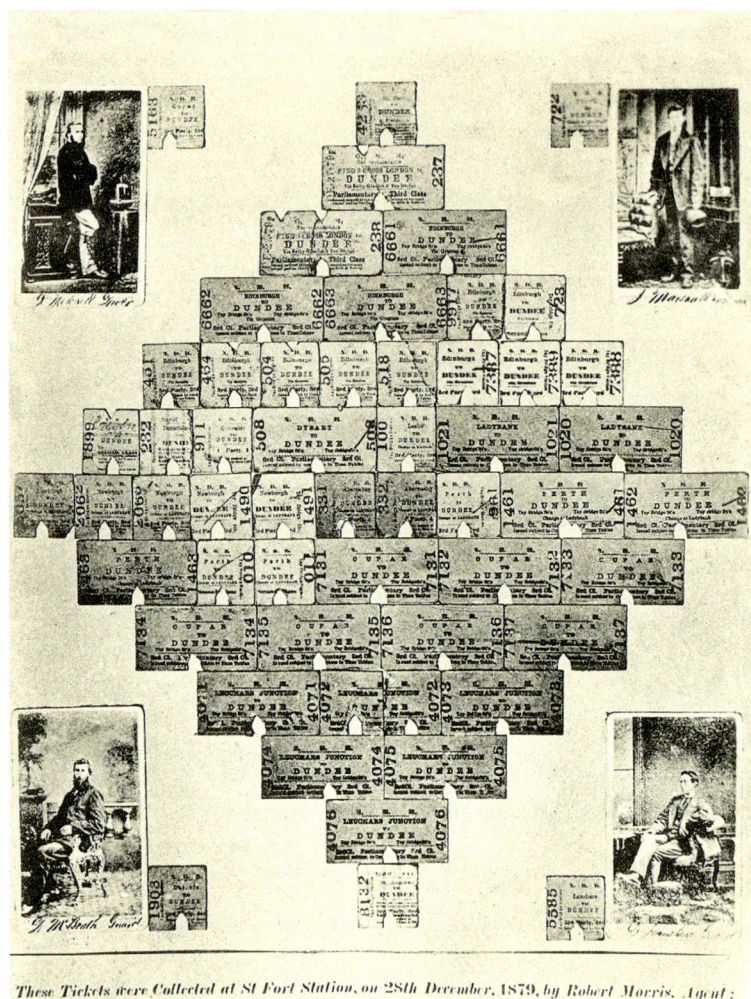

the 'news pictures' of the day. In the days before even fixed line telephones became commonplace, the postcard was the quickest, cheapest and most popular means of communication amongst friends and family, and thus lent it itself easily to the dissemination of illustrated news stories. The disaster postcard, therefore, became a global phenomenon, a routine part of the general public's ability to access news.

Many examples have been located from publishers in the USA, France, Germany, Belgium, Panama and elsewhere. Demand for these cards must

left: One of the many contemporary illustrations of the scene the morning after the Tay Bridge Disaster in December 1879.

have been considerable. After the Miraflores disaster in Panama, a series of tinted cards was produced by a local publisher, and the economics of printing in colour could only have been justified by massive sales.

In Britain, a pioneer in the production of photo-composite cards of disasters was Warner Gothard of Barnsley, and there was hardly a major fatal mining, road transport or railway accident between 1905 and 1916 which did not feature in their catalogue. Examples of their cards can be

below: Part of the collapsed section of the bridge after it was retrieved from the bed of the River Tay with one of the carriages from the stricken train still trapped within its structure.

right: The locomotive involved in the Tay Bridge disaster – a North British Railway (NBR), Wheatley-designed Class 224 4-4-0 No.224 built in 1871 – was raised from the river bed in May 1890, rebuilt at Cowlairs, and returned to service. Nicknamed 'The Diver' thereafter, it was scrapped in 1919. A 1904 'Elco Series' postcard, re-using one of Valentine's 1880 images.

below right: The tender was also rescued from the river bed and re-used.

found throughout this book, and today these cards, and composites by other publishers, are highly collectible, and informative historical documents in their own right. Words can set the scene but, as they say, a photograph is worth a thousand words. Surviving photographs and postcards, when seen alongside the official Board of Trade enquiries which followed every major incident, present a fascinating record of the causes of the accidents, and the many changes in operating procedures which followed.

The outcome of that 1898 Wellingborough accident for example – *illustrated on page 13* – directly led to widespread modifications, limiting the maximum permitted slope of a platform.

Accidents were more frequent in the closing years of the 19th century and the early years of the 20th than today, and while some resulted from driver error, most were equipment failures – often brakes failing to reduce

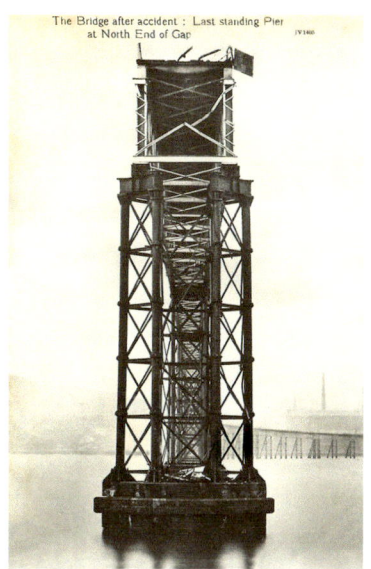

above left: One of the bridge piers left standing after the central section collapsed. Another 1879 image marketed as a postcard in 1904.

above: In contrast, a fragment of one of the remaining piers of the old bridge is sharply contrasted with the robustness of its replacement.

speed quickly enough. Railway infrastructure was much less sophisticated and, with so many independent companies, it was even more fragmented than today, and the quest for speed between competing companies was cited as the main cause of many accidents. Lest you might think 'ambulance-chasing' and 'papparazzi' are modern phenomena, the alacrity with which photographs were published, showing the results of trains colliding at speed, was remarkable. The postcard became a news medium.

As postcard collecting became one of the most popular crazes of the early 20th century, worldwide, photographic studios dipped into their archives to find new subjects to sell to collectors. When Thomas Bouch's Tay Bridge infamously collapsed during a storm on 28 December 1879, one of Scotland's leading photographic studios – James Valentine & Son of Dundee – were close at hand, and pictures of the bridge with the great gap where the collapsed section had once stood were on sale relatively quickly after the event.

Such was the demand for photographic postcards a quarter of a century after Valentines had taken the photographs, they would finally reach a wide audience with the company's decision to re-issue many of them as postcards. By that time, the craze for collecting postcards was in the ascendancy, and photographic studios seized the opportunity to check through their files and dust off their old negatives, with a view to giving them a second – and usually highly profitable – lease of life.

Today, most of the surviving postcards have never seen the inside of a postbox, bought new as collectibles to be preserved in albums rather than posted. All but a few of the illustrations in this book are from postcards.

John Hannavy, Great Cheverell 2026

1900 – A DISASTROUS START TO A NEW CENTURY

below: The collision in Slough Station on 16 June was caused by the driver of a Great Western Railway (G.W.R.) train passing a danger signal. Five people died, 35 suffered serious injuries and at least 90 others were hurt.

The photographic postcard era was still just in the future when the 20th century opened. In the century's first year there were no fewer than 72 railway accidents considered serious enough to warrant official reports to the Board of Trade. The first two of those occurred on New Year's Day at Ashbourne in Derbyshire and on the North Eastern Railway (NER) at Monkseaton, to the last of the year at Ropley in Hampshire on 27 December.

Given the combination of relatively flimsy wooden-bodied carriages, primitive signalling and often inadequate or inefficient brakes, it is remarkable that there were relatively few fatalities amongst the passengers

above and left: On 24 July 1900, the driver and one passenger were killed when a Lancashire & Yorkshire Railway (L&Y.R) express carrying holidaymakers back from Blackpool to Leeds left the track at Amberswood Junction near Wigan. Twenty-five others were injured – fewer than might have been expected given the steep embankment down which the train fell. The photographs were taken by Crippen & Company whose studio was at No.2 Spring Bank in Pemberton, and who would open a second studio in Wigan's Market Square the following year. In the days before photographic postcards, hand-made prints were available for purchase.

and train crews in all those accidents. In all the collisions and derailments which were subject to Board of Trade reports that year, 32 people lost their lives and well over 700 were injured – some of them were train crew, most were passengers – the exact figure remains uncertain either because of incomplete reporting, or only partial records, and those figures are almost certain to be a serious under-estimate. But according to records in the National Railway Museum, in 1900 alone more than 16,000 railway employees across the separate railway companies in the country were either injured or killed in the course of their work – a shocking indictment. By 1913 that annual number had risen to over 30,000. Workforce safety had clearly not yet started to be taken seriously.

The Amberswood Junction disaster *illustrated above* was one of the many crashes caused by a combination of faults and errors – equipment failure and drivers failing to observe required procedures setting off a chain of events with disastrous consequences.

Amberswood Junction was quite a complex junction, with several lines either merging or crossing each other within a short distance. After a relative straight run from Standish signal box just over four miles away, the driver should have reduced his speed almost to a walking pace before negotiating a tight curve (with no guide rail) as he approached the junction. He was estimated to be travelling at a minimum of 30mph as he approached the points. Add a damaged rail into the equation and the accident was inevitable. But one of the most astounding conclusions by the inspector – Lieutenant-Colonel P. G von Donop, whose name will feature many times in this book – the track in question was so worn by heavy use that, in the 14 years since it was laid in 1886, it had lost at least 20% of its weight and was thus severely weakened.

In so many of the accidents recorded for 1900, one major issue stands out – brake failure, or inadequate braking power, may not have been the actual cause of the collision or derailment, but it was found to have been a major contributory factor in the seriousness of the outcome.

Records show that two successive accidents – on 1 October and 7 October – both on the London & South Western Railway (L&SWR), the first at Virginia Water Station, the second at Twickenham.

The Virginia Water collision occurred when a signalman gave the 'clear' signal to a train hauling horse boxes, having forgotten that there was an empty passenger train – which he could see from his signal box – standing at the up platform. In the collision, both drivers were injured, and the passenger train's guard was killed. The Coroner's report, while blaming the signalman, made an interesting observation regarding the horse-box train's driver:

> 'The fact that he was driving bunker in front may explain why he did not recognize more quickly the position of the train in front of him. It appears to me that the mere fact of a man's work necessitating the frequent turning of his back to the direction in which his engine is running, must militate against the maintenance of a good look-out.'

Signalling confusion was also deemed to be the major factor in the Twickenham accident just six days later – with apparently unclear and contradictory instructions being issued by the signalman, the station master, and a railway inspector, as some shunting of occupied coaches from one train to another was undertaken. Fifty-one people were injured as a result

It was already clear as the new century got underway, that the railway network was still a dangerous place to be, whether as a passenger or, more strikingly, a an employee.

1901 – THE FIRST POSTCARDS OF RAILWAY ACCIDENTS

Showing the early stages of the recovery of a locomotive after a derailment at Gretna Station in 1901, the postcard below is the earliest photographic postcard in this book. When pictorial cards were first given approval by the Post Office, strict rules were enforced – so a white space for a brief message – usually no more than one or two lines – was left beneath the photograph in early pictorial cards. This card has an 'undivided back', and that means it conformed to official rules in 1901.

Everything changed in early 1902 when Britain became the first country in the world to approve the use of 'divided back' postcards – which permitted the message to be written on the left and the address on the right, the format which we use today.

For a time that new freedom imposed a new restriction – until other countries adopted the protocol, British divided back cards could not be posted overseas, and were therefore of no use to foreign tourists visiting Britain. It would, for example, be 1907 before the US Postal Service would accept divided back cards.

below: The image used on this postcard is likely to have been photographed on the day of the Gretna accident itself as the clear-up has not yet been started. The space below the picture was for the sender's message, with only the address being permitted on the reverse.

below: On 18 May 1901, a temporary ramp of stacked sleepers and rails was used to chain-haul the Glasgow & South Western Railway's 4-4-0 express engine No.57 back on to the track. A temporary balustrade – also made of sleepers – had been built on the bridge to keep the crowd at bay. This postcard was on sale both in monochrome and tinted, the coloured version being an early, and seldom repeated, extravagance. The 'divided back' card carries a postmark of 5 December 1902, 18 months after the derailment.

The 8.20pm Caledonian Railway (CR) goods train from Gushetfaulds – a goods yard in the Mount Florida area of Glasgow – hauling 44 waggons and a brake van to Carlisle, was partially derailed as it approached Gretna Junction on the 'up' main line in the early hours of 14 May, some of the derailed waggons slewing across the 'down' line into the path of the 1.15am double-headed G&SWR goods train from Carlisle, bound for Glasgow hauling 22 waggons and a brake van. The pilot engine on the G&SWR train was 4-4-0 express engine No.57 being returned to Glasgow, with locomotive No.364, an 0-6-0 goods engine as the train engine. The Caledonian locomotive involved in the accident was 0-6-0 goods engine No.461. The cause of the accident was attributed to the uneven loading of 'cylindrical steel forgings' on one of the waggons, causing that waggon to leave the track on a bend while the train was travelling at a mere 28 mph. Perhaps unusually, the official report concluded that:

> 'No blame whatever rests upon the drivers, foremen or brakemen of the two trains. The working was correct, the signals were lowered for both trains, and there is no reason for supposing the speed of either train was too high.'

This may be the first British railway accident to have appeared on postcards, establishing the tradition which would, over the years, become a significant source of historical record.

1902 – 'I FEARED IF I SAID ANYTHING I WOULD CAUSE A PANIC'

That was the admission was part of the evidence given to the Board of Trade Inquiry by Mr. J. Linstead, a passenger in one of the heavily overcrowded third-class carriages on the 06.50 commuter train from Chingford to London Liverpool Street on 25 April 1902 after he had heard a loud bump and felt a severe jolt as the train passed through Clapton Tunnel. He added that:

> '... from that point we ran bumping along the sleepers. The bumping continued until we reached a point about half-way between the mouth of the tunnel and the station. At this point, the carriage appeared to leave the metals entirely. We went on travelling over the sleepers until the sudden crash came, and the carriage in which I was riding seemed to bump into the one in front of it, and the passengers in my compartment appeared to be shot out the reverse side, and the carriage commenced to break up and to topple over on to its side.'

below: There appear to be no photographs surviving of the Hackney Downs accident – nor indeed is there any evidence that any were ever taken – and just this one postcard of the station dating from a few years later.

Given his account of what occurred inside that carriage as it broke up, any attempt to avoid causing a panic would have been rather futile.

Several other passengers gave similar horrendous accounts to the official enquiry into the accident – in which three died and 197 were injured – but as the carriages had no communication cords, they had been unable to alert the train crew.

The train was being hauled by a Great Eastern Railway (GER) R24 tank engine running 'bunker first' and consisted of 15 coaches carrying about 700 passengers – most of them in seven overcrowded 3rd Class carriages. One of the carriages had suffered a broken axle – due to an invisible flaw in its casting – and was derailed as it approached the station. At the time, the GER was in the process of fitting 'communication cords' to all its carriage stock, but this set of ageing 6-wheeled non-corridor coaches had not yet been updated. Later in the decade, such an accident would have drawn postcard photographers like a magnet, but research has so far failed to reveal any such cards of this incident.

There were just under 700 passengers and train crew injured in the 48 accidents for which Board of Trade reports were produced during 1902, but that, again, almost certainly under-estimates the true figure. The number of fatalities listed in those reports, at just seven, meant that the year stands out as being the railways' best in terms of the period covered by this book. 1902 and 1908 were the only two years in which the death tolls published in those accident reports remained in single figures.

There were, however, some spectacular accidents which, given the damage done to the rolling stock and trackbed, might have been expected to cost more lives than they did. Added to that the apparent lack of any postcards of the aftermath of those accidents, makes the 1902 publication of that coloured postcard of the 1901 Gretna derailment, discussed on the previous pages, all the more notable.

The first three months of the year had seen only relatively minor accidents – starting with four injured in the accident near Pendleton Station on the Lancashire & Yorkshire Railway. But April saw one person die and 58 injured in a London & North Western Railway (L&NWR) accident at Sutton Coldfield. May's worst was 23 injured in the G&SWR accident at Kilmarnock, and then the next large number of casualties was experienced at Glasgow's Charing Cross Station. Thirty-eight people were injured on the NER at Harrogate on 5 September, and 80 in the GER accident at Brentwood on 20 November.

Photographers and postcard publishers appear to have been inactive in all of those, while elsewhere in the world, 'disaster postcards' were already gaining popularity. Was there still a residual British sensitivity towards such blatant portrayal of death and injury, perhaps still considered to be an inappropriate and ghoulish fascination?

The Charing Cross crash was blamed on a signalling error – the signalman sending the 'line clear' message to the wrong signal box – which allowed the 07.55 workman's train from Helensburgh to run into the back of the 08.05 train from Kilsyth which was standing at the up platform. According to the Board of Trade report, 'the Helensburgh train was horsed by a four-wheels-coupled leading bogie, tender engine, chimney in front'. That was a popular figure of speech used by Major J. W. Pringle in his reports. While photographers do not seem to have attended the wreckage, artists from *The Illustrated London News* recreated the scene of the wreckage, together with an inset illustration of the station master trying to stop the approaching Kilmarnock train. All of the injured were on the Kilsyth train.

The cover of *The Illustrated London News* for 6 September 1902. Signalling errors and lack of care by the driver of the Helensburgh train were both deemed to have contributed to the disaster.

"You will have heard of our railway disaster – you can only see part of the horror here" wrote 'Mab' to Miss Cross of Winsford on 21 July 1903 on the first of these cards. The impact with the station footbridge caused major damage to the bridge – visible on the left of the picture – requiring its demolition. Hartley Brothers' studio was at 2 South Road, Waterloo, Liverpool. Their postcard business offered cards of the disaster in two qualities – this simple letterpress example being the cheaper. The more expensive version (*middle*) was printed by lithography with red captioning. Such was local interest that at least 12 different postcards of the disaster were on sale within a week of it occurring.

HARTLEY BROS.
Photo. Copyright.

Railway Disaster at Waterloo Station, July 15th, 1903.

Copyright—Hartley Bros., Waterloo.

Railway Disaster, Waterloo Station, July 15th, 1903.

Published by T. REYNOLDS, WATERLOO.

Waterloo Railway Disaster, Wednesday, July 15th, 1903.

1903 – 'OUR EPIDEMIC OF RAILWAY DISASTERS'

So serious were some of the accidents in 1903, according to contemporary coverage, that the illustrated journal *The Graphic* ran an editorial feature on the rescue and clear-up operations after a number of them, titled 'Our Epidemic of Railway Disasters'. And yet, 1903 was by no means the worst year in the first decade of the century. While certainly much worse than 1902, there would be years when the price paid by passengers and crew was of a much higher order. Perhaps it was the contrast with 1902 which prompted that headline, or perhaps it was the growing number of photographs and postcards of rail disasters which amplified public disquiet over safety.

One of those disasters was the extensively-photographed derailment of a L&YR passenger train after striking the footbridge at Waterloo

below: This view of the aftermath of the accident at Liverpool's Waterloo Station was taken by yet another local photographer – Ellis Vernon Empson, whose Sandringham Studio, was at Sandringham Road in Waterloo. Today that is a predominantly residential street.

top: Local people take part in the rescue and clear-up.

middle: The distorted wreckage of the 'Lanky Tank' – No.670 – which had been running 'chimney first' when the derailment took place. The impact with the station footbridge was so great that the locomotive finished up on the platform and facing the wrong way.

bottom: The damaged station footbridge which later had to be demolished.

Railway Disaster at Waterloo Station, July 15th, 1903.
RIMMER'S LIBRARY SERIES, WATERLOO.

The Wrecked Engine, No. 670.
THE RAILWAY DISASTER, WATERLOO, JULY 15TH, 1903.

HARTLEY BROS. Photo. Copyright.
Railway Disaster at Waterloo Station, July 15th, 1903.

station in Liverpool on 15 July. At least four local publishers – all of them based in the Waterloo area of Liverpool – quickly sent photographers to the scene, and three of them had series of postcards of the wreckage on sale in local shops within days. Of the postcards illustrated here, the earliest was posted just six days after the accident had taken place.

The train was reported to have approached a tight bend at the station much too fast, the resulting accident costing seven lives, with 112 people injured. The official report gave a detailed description of the train:

> 'The 4.30 p.m. express from Liverpool to Southport was derailed just as it was approaching Waterloo Station on the down line. The train consisted of a four-wheels-coupled tank engine with a radial axle at each end, travelling chimney first, and of six bogie carriages, the first and last being third brakes with the brake compartment of the first carriage next the engine. The automatic vacuum brake was in use on the train, actuating blocks on the four coupled wheels of the engine and on all the carriage wheels.
>
> Six passengers and the fireman were killed or have since died, and 112 passengers and the driver and three other servants of the Company were injured.'

For passengers travelling in wooden-bodied coaches, accidents inevitably resulted in serious injuries and deaths. Sometime after the report was published, a seventh person died from their injuries.

The locomotive at the head of the train – seen heavily deformed in the postcard, *middle left* – was one of John Aspinall's Horwich-built 2-4-2 tank engines, known as 'Lanky Tanks' which were regular L&YR workhorses. 270 of them were built between 1889 and 1901. A sole survivor of the class, No.1008 – the first locomotive to be built at the L&YR's new Horwich Locomotive Works – is preserved in the National Railway Museum in York.

In addition to the Waterloo disaster, there were 32 others that year, considered to be serious enough to warrant an official investigation resulting in a further 25 deaths and over 500 injuries. Despite the headline in *The Graphic*, this was actually not an unusual tally.

The year's most serious incident occurred on 27 July at St. Enoch's Station in Glasgow and was attributed to a combination of driver error and excessive speed, when a G&SWR train ran into the station and its brakes proved insufficient to bring it to a halt. It telescoped into the platform-end buffers. Sixteen died and 64 were injured.

On 27 February an entire FR train overturned on the Leven Viaduct between Ulverston and Grange-over-Sands in a severe gale. The 49-span, 480 metre (0.3 miles) viaduct carried the line between Barrow and

right: Postcards of the accident at Penrith Station were not produced to a very high print quality, suggesting, perhaps, that widespread sales were not anticipated. This card shows the damaged locomotive from the passenger train, standing at the 'up' platform at Penrith Station. The damage was described as: 'Buffer plank broken to pieces; cylinder front broken; smoke box front knocked in; blast pipe knocked out; tube ends damaged; front right-hand framing badly damaged, left hand slightly; coupling rods dent; ashpan bottom knocked in; firebar carrier broken; hopper and cylinder cocks knocked off; engine steps both sides knocked off; internal chimney broken; grease pipe broken off at nipple; sand valve nozzle broken left side'.

bottom: The passenger train's tender being craned away.

Carnforth just 8 metres above the water level. Originally built in the 1840s – using cast iron pillars carrying wrought iron spans – the viaduct had been rebuilt in 1880. It would be rebuilt again in 1915 when the cast iron columns would be encased in brick. The official report noted that

> 'In this case as the 4.25 a.m. down mail passenger train from Carnforth to Barrow was standing on the viaduct all the vehicles on the train, 10 in number, were overturned on to the up line during a terrific gale. All the passengers in the train, 34 in number, were injured, but only one is reported as being in a serious condition. The two guards were also injured, one rather severely, and one Post Office sorting clerk.'

The wrecked Express at Penrith Station, Dec. 5th, 1903.

The wrecked Express at Penrith Station, Dec. 5th, 1903.

Initially it was reported that some passengers had been lost in the river, but that was later proved to be untrue. It was not until 5 March that newspapers carried the full story, reporting that immediately after the accident

> '… it became evident that four persons, a man, a woman, and two children, who had certainly been in the train, were missing. As it was impossible that they could have voluntarily moved far away, there is little doubt that as the carriage in which they were riding was hurled off the track they were precipitated through the opened door into the swollen River Leven below.… … It was considered improbable that any of the passengers had gone amissing. The hats found in one of the carriages which gave rise to the rumour have been claimed.'

The collision at Penrith Station which occurred on 5 December 1903, however, was one of the more bizarre Edwardian railway accidents – a combination of equipment failure, bad decision-making, and really bad timing led to an accident which could have had a much more serious outcome. Nobody on the L&NWR express was seriously hurt, but reading the official accident report published on 3 February 1904, it could so easily have been otherwise.

> 'In this case, the 8.10 p.m. goods train from Liverpool to Carlisle became divided as it was approaching Penrith Station. The driver, on reaching the station, improperly stopped the first portion of the train, causing the rear portion to come into violent collision with it, with the result that several waggons were wrecked, and one or more of them thrown on to the up line. At that instant the 1 a.m. express train from Carlisle to London reached the place, and collided with the waggons which were foul of the up line.'

The express was totally destroyed, but there were no fatalities. The express driver was severely scalded and his fireman suffered bruises. Driver error was blamed as he had ignored Rule 220 which stated:

> 'The engine driver, on seeing a green signal waved slowly from side to side from a signal box, must understand that his train is divided, and must exercise great caution by looking out for the second portion, and, unless he has reason to believe the line is not clear ahead, must *not stop the portion attached to his engine* until he is satisfied that the rear portion has been stopped, or is moving very slowly.'

1904 – 'A SINGULAR MISHAP'

Not all railway accidents result in loss of life – however dramatic the photographs of them might be. Some just look worse than they actually were. The accident at Albany Road in Coventry on 4 July 1904 was one such event, reported in detail in The *Midland Daily Telegraph* that same day, albeit illustrated with a line drawing rather than a photograph.

'A singular mishap occurred early this morning on the London and North Western Railway at Coventry, several coaches falling over an embankment. Fortunately, no one was injured, but considerable damage was done to the carriages. It appears that some coaches were left standing on the temporary siding near Albany Road, these being intended for use with an excursion train which was

below: The task of recovering the four coaches spread across Albany Road, Coventry, was in progress within hours of the event. Large crowds had gathered, drawn by rumours of serious casualties – thankfully unfounded. The breakdown gang quickly laid a temporary track (inset), and the last carriage had been hauled back up the embankment by 3.30pm that afternoon.

Smash of the "FLYING WELSHMAN," October 3rd, 1904.—*Copyright.*

to leave Coventry at 4.55am for Blackpool. The engine which was to work the train entered the siding with the other coaches for the purpose of drawing out those already in the siding. The two sets of carriages came in contact with each other, and before they could be secured four of the coaches started to run backwards. Ultimately these ran down the embankment into Albany Road. The heavy weight of the carriages caused the first to mount the footpath on the opposite side of the road. Happily, the houses escaped the impact; otherwise a serious disaster must have occurred. The noise caused by the falling carriages was considerable and created a sensation in the neighbourhood. The rear of one of the coaches was smashed in, the buffers of another were broken, and the carriages were more or less damaged. The mishap, bad as it was, caused no delay to the excursion, however, as other carriages were procured. A breakdown gang was at once sent for, and the work of removing the damaged coaches was soon commenced.'

Such a speedy resolution would be highly unlikely to happen today, as numerous Health and Safety issues would have to be dealt with before the bridge could be re-opened.

A major accident occurred at Bacus Marsh between Bynea and Loughor near Lllanelli on 3 October 1904 when the double-headed

above: One of the many postcards produced after the 'Flying Welshman' accident, which oddly name the train but not the location. The double-headed train was hauled by 1886-built GWR Dean-designed 0-6-0 saddle tank No. 1674 ahead of the 6-month old 'Bulldog Class' 4-4-0 tender locomotive No. 3460 *Montreal*. The tank engine had only been added to the train at Llanelli to assist in the long climb up the two and a half mile, 1 in 50, Cockett Bank. Both locomotives were overturned, but later repaired and returned t service, *Montreal* only being disposed of in September 1935. As well as the destruction of much of the train, the derailment destroyed more than 70 yards of track. No lesser figure than George Jackson Churchward suggested to the enquiry that the use of the 'unsuitable' tank engine probably contributed to the disaster.

The 'Flying Welshman' recovery underway, with cranes brought in from all over south Wales.

Smash of the "FLYING WELSHMAN," October 3rd, 1904.—*Copyright.*

This photograph was taken by Jack Lewis, whose studio was at 9a Castle Bailey Street, Swansea. Whilst the damage to the train was considerable, the official enquiry noted that 'Had the rolling-stock been constructed with wooden instead of steel underframes, it is probable that the greater portion of the train would have been smashed to pieces.'

'Flying Welshman' GWR mail train from Milford Haven to London Paddington was derailed, resulting in 5 deaths and 94 injured. Known variously as the 'Llanelly disaster' the 'Loughor disaster' the 'Bynea disaster' and the 'G.W.R. Disaster', the accident was extensively covered by local photographers, with several series of postcards of the aftermath being published.

The Board of Trade enquiry was inconclusive as to the primary cause, but suggested poor maintenance, old rolling stock, excessive speed, the use of an inappropriate banking engine may all have contributed.

G.W.R. Disaster. Llanelly, Oct. 3rd, 1904.

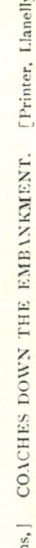

George Jackson Churchward told the enquiry that the saddle tank was designed to run at a maximum of 50 mph, and so was operating at a speed beyond its safety limit. The enquiry suggested that the banker should be added at the foot of Cockett Bank rather than more than two miles back along a level straight section of track. In the light of this accident, the enquiry recommended that a working party of all interested railway companies be established to look into the issues of tank engines being used as bankers.

above: This postcard gives no clue to the location, apart from the fact that it was printed and published in Llanelli. It gives a good sense of the embankment down which the train rolled. In the official report it was suggested that the train may have been travelling at about 60 mph, rather than the designated 50 mph, at the time of the derailment.

left: This view of the Aylesbury disaster on 23 December 1904 gives a most comprehensive impression of just how devastating the impact in the derailment must have been. The wreckage of GCR Class 11b locomotive No.1040, running from London Marylebone Street to Manchester, lies on its side to the right of the picture. Excessive speed was blamed.

above: This postcard of the wreckage after the GCR accident on 23 December 1904 at Aylesbury still includes a message space to the left of the photograph.

right: From the opposite end of the station to the view on page 37, this view of the Aylesbury wreckage was photographed and published by Samuel Glendenning Payne – trading as S. G. Payne & Son – of 43 High Street, Aylesbury. To the left is Class 11B No.1042 which was hauling a southbound train and was slightly damaged when it collided with the wreckage.

1904's last accident – on 23 December – occurred when the almost-empty 10-coach 02.45 train from Marylebone to Manchester Central was derailed in fog having entered a tight curve at speed and then mounted the platform on its approach to Aylesbury Station. Four died and four were injured, all of them Great Central Railway (GCR) employees, and the only people on the train. Had the train been busier, the toll of death and injury would inevitably have been higher. A southbound train then ploughed into the wreckage.

1905 – PHOTOGRAPHERS WERE QUICKLY ON THE SCENE

Almost half of the 51 people who died in railway accidents during 1905 lost their lives at Hall Road Station, Blundellsands, between Formby and Bootle on Thursday 27 July when, due to a signalling error, the 16.30 Liverpool to Southport train ran into an empty local train standing in the Middle Siding at Hall Road Station on the L&YR's recently electrified line. Twenty of the 78 passengers and crew died. All the fatalities were third-class passengers travelling in the leading 'Third Class Motor Car' of the express. The motorman and a further 47 passengers were injured, one of whom subsequently died from his injuries.

According to the official report, the empty local train had been shunted into the Middle Siding to allow the express to pass, but the

below: The wrecked bodywork of Third-Class Motor Car No.3015 on the local train.

inset: this message was sent to Kitty Ballantyne on 4 August 1905 using the postcard of the Hall Road wreckage.

right: The aftermath of the Hall Road collision, showing a tarpaulin over coach No.3015 the lead driving car of the stationary local train which was almost totally destroyed in the collision. The driving bogies of 3015 finished up underneath the bodywork of the third-class car, 3105, nearest the camera. The remaining three cars were First-Class Trailer Cars 422 and 411, and Third-Class Motor Car 3009.

below: A tarpaulin covers the remains of the lead driving car of the stationary local train, while both of its driving bogies – normally at either end of the motor car – have been driven underneath the bodywork of the third-class car, 3105, giving a very real sense of the force of the impact.

points had failed to close properly and the signalman was unable to clear the signal for the express. He then tried to free the points working them back and forth three times but, unable to change the signal, had waved a green flag for the driver of the express – who understandably read that as a signal to proceed, and accelerated his train. The signalman had, however, left the points set for the siding and the express was diverted into it at increasing speed, ploughing into the rear of the stationary train at speed. The lead motor car of the express and the lead motor car of

After removing motor car 3051, work starts on clearing the tracks, while another electric set passes on the down line on its way south to Liverpool.

the local train were effectively both demolished as the impact telescoped them together – pushing the body of the front motor car of the express inside the body of the stationary train's lead motor car – and pushing the 170-ton local train 50 metres down the track.

Photographers from at least three postcard publishers were on the scene even before the clean-up started, and the first series of postcards – photographed and published by 'Newcombe' of St. John's Road in Waterloo, Liverpool – were on sale early the week after. One such card, (see page 39), was posted to an address in County Antrim on 4 August, carrying the message 'This p.C. [*sic*] is of the smash on the L+Y last week I told you about.' Today that would have been sent instantaneously by WhatsApp.

Catering for the different purchasing powers of his customers, Newcombe produced his cards in two distinct qualities – 'real photographs' like the one here, and cheaper letterpress-printed black and white cards

The line had been electrified by the Lancashire & Yorkshire Railway just the previous year, using a 625-volt DC 4-rail system, and the original 4-car sets had two power cars, each with two 150hp motors. By the beginning of 1905, however, new and much more powerful – and faster – 5-car sets had been introduced, and the service comprised seven trains an hour from Liverpool – one express and three slower stopping trains to Southport, and three local services only running as far as Hall Road. Electrification meant the journey time of stopping trains to Southport had reduced from 54 minutes under steam down to 37 minutes.

The new 5-car electric sets, on heavy steel underframes, had been built in Horwich at the L&YR's works there, and the electrical traction systems had been built in Preston by Dick, Kerr & Company. They were the first such vehicles to see service in Britain.

Perhaps unusually, the majority of the postcards published of the Huddersfield disaster were produced, not by one of the large postcard companies, but by a gifted local amateur photographer named Smith Carter. Of the victims, the two who were killed and nine of the passengers, were all on a local L&YR train. The crews of both trains were also injured. The effect of the 90-ton L&NWR locomotive hitting the incoming train was to telescope three coaches, completely destroying the second one.

Carter had held various jobs – blacksmith, fireman, railway porter – and eventually turned his amateur passion for photography into a small postcard business, every postcard presumably being hand-printed in his own darkroom. Five years after his success with the Huddersfield train crash postcards, he turned professional, operating as a 'photographer and wholesale dealer' until bankruptcy befell him in 1926.

Both of the trains involved in the accident were the newer 5-car electric sets and all the fatalities were in the leading third-class motor car of the Southport-bound express. The local train was made up of a leading third-class motor car, another third class car, two first class cars, and a third class motor car at the rear, the order being reversed on the express.

In his report to the Board of Trade published on 2 September, the Inspector, Lieut-Col E. Druitt, cited signalling errors, driver error and possibly points failure amongst the many factors which he believed had contributed to the accident.

He also drew attention to a number of emerging and extremely important points about the differences between the traditional protocols and procedures between operating an electric railway compared with a steam-hauled railway, concluding that:

> 'Looking at the facts connected with the collision, the two most striking results are, first, the absence of any fire among the derailed coaches, the danger from fire being one regarded as especially liable to occur on railways using electric traction and, secondly, the very small amount of damage done to the cars, with the exception of the leading car of each train, due no doubt to the very heavy and stiff underframes.
>
> Probably the collision would not have been so severe if steam locomotives had been in use, as under the same conditions the acceleration of the express would not have been so rapid; that on the electric trains is stated to be such that a speed of 30 miles an hour can be obtained from rest in a period of 30 seconds, but this, and the quick stopping due to the very powerful brakes in use, form the great advantages of electric traction for a fast and frequent passenger service of trains, and no danger need result therefrom if the ordinary rules for working trains are adhered to.'

A couple of days after the accident, local newspaper The *Bootle Herald* had told a very different story in its report of 29 July

> 'The disaster was one of the most appalling in the history of such calamitous events, for on the collision of the trains, the coaches concerned immediately set fire and the scene was so awful as to baffle a description of its horrors. People were wedged in under the burning wreckage, and it was impossible for a long time to extricate them. Indeed, the first task was to get the flames subdued.'

While it is true that there were small localised fires, the people first on the scene had quickly extinguished them, and by the time the local fire

Warner Gothard of Barnsley's first photo-composite 'disaster' postcards were on sale just a few days after the 19 January collision. Three different composites were produced of the accident, none of them printed to the standard of the studio's later series. (*Mark Fynn / www.warnergothard.com*)

This view, by the Barnsley Photo Co, is one of several they published as postcards. This was clearly taken within minutes of the upper right-hand image on the Gothard card, *opposite,* and from a very similar camera position, albeit using a different, wide-angle, lens.

Midland Railway 1897-built 4-4-0 locomotive No.154 lying on its side after the Cudworth disaster. The Derby-built locomotive was being used as the pilot engine on the London-bound express. Behind, the Samuel-Johnson-designed Class 3 'Belpaire' 4-4-0 No.833 was the train's driving engine, built in Derby in 1903.

brigades arrived they were no longer needed. The journal *The Engineer*, in the editorial in its issue for 4 February was quick to criticise the national media for inaccurate reporting –

> 'It may be stated here at once that electricity had nothing whatever to do with the accident. It has been stated in the columns of the daily press that the train was set on fire by the current. Nothing of the kind took place. The moment the collision occurred the magnetic fuse in the power-house was "blown". A second afterwards some iron falling on the up line made a short circuit, and the fuse for that road "blew" so that almost as soon as the accident happened the line became "dead".'

The first two fatal accidents to occur in 1905 had happened on 17 and 19 January – both of them in the early hours of the morning, but their causes and outcomes were very different. On 17 January, one person had died and another was injured near Howden on the North Eastern Railway as a result of a signalling error in fog resulting in the collision between a goods train and a mineral train.

In the official report on the disaster at Cudworth on the Midland Railway, which occurred two days later, the cause was officially described as human error – the driver passing a signal at danger. Seven died and 18 were injured but, by all accounts, it could have been very much worse

below: In this view of the clear-up after the Cudworth crash, by the Barnsley Photo Co, a rival photographer – taking pictures for Warner Gothard perhaps? – is setting up his camera.

SCOTCH EXPRESS COLLISION, CUDWORTH   Barnsley Photo Co

below: Another Barnsley Photo Co card showing the total destruction of some of the wooden-bodied coaching stock.

'In this case the 2.25 a.m. up mail train (Leeds to Sheffield) was travelling between Cudworth and Darfield stations, when the 3.5 a.m. up express train (Leeds to St. Pancras) running at high speed overtook it. The result was a tail-end collision with disastrous effects. Four passengers, a railway guard and a fireman, all of whom were in the express, were killed on the spot.

Thirteen passengers, of whom one has since died from the effects of injuries received, and five railway employees suffered more or less severely from shock or injury.

One of the vehicles of the mail train, a fish truck, was derailed by the collision, and came to rest foul of the down main line. A third train, the midnight down express (St. Pancras to Carlisle), before it could be brought to a standstill, came into slight contact with this truck. No one fortunately was seriously injured by this second collision, and but little further damage resulted.'

Cudworth was also the first incident to become the subject of one of Warner Gothard of Barnsley's 'disaster' cards – although the standard of their first two postcards was well below the studio's later photo-composite productions.

While Gothards are known to have published three postcards of the disaster, the local postcard publisher which styled itself the Barnsley Photo Co, but gave no address, produced at least six different views, four of which

above: A rare photo-composite postcard of the Witham crash, produced by the Duyshart studio of 75 Duke Street, Chelmsford – operated at the time by Alida Duyshart, widow of the founder, Pieter Johannes Duyshart. This is the only photo-composite card of a rail crash not by Warner Gothard discovered so far during the research for this project.

are included on these pages. The similarity between the photographs which appeared on the two publishers' card is strongly suggestive of them being taken at the same time. For the state of the fire in the Barnsley Photo Co card and the top right image in the Warner Gothard composite – *see previous pages* – to be so similar, suggests the two photographs must have been taken within no more than a few minutes of each other. While Warner Gothard was, himself, an accomplished photographer, he frequently acquired images from other photographers for his composite cards.

left: The wreckage at Witham Station, photographed by Fred Spalding Jnr of Chelmsford, who had taken over his late father's photographic studio.

The devastation at Witham station shortly after the accident, with many of the coaches reduced to matchsticks. These dramatic postcards were the news pictures of their day. Just a few years later, journalistic images like this would be seen on the front pages of daily newspapers.

A postcard by Lankester & Co. of Tunbridge Wells, from a series this time showing part of the wreckage of the Cromer express, underneath the station footbridge.

The wreck of the GER's 09.27 Cromer Express from London Liverpool Street, which occurred at Witham on 1 September 1905, was deemed to have had multiple causes, and led to 11 deaths and more than 70 injured. The cause was probably a combination of a defective length of track, and some obstacle on the track from ongoing plate-laying. A number of photographers were quickly on the scene, and the wreckage became the subject of more than a dozen postcards.

Also extensively photographed (*see page 42*) was the accident which occurred at Huddersfield station on Good Friday 1905 – 21 April – an accident which should never have been possible. At 13.50 that afternoon, a two-coach L&NWR train, which was being shunted out of Huddersfield Station, collided with an express train arriving from Bradford. The first

From Fred Spalding's series, a group of workmen gather around one of the derailed coaches – are they part of the clear-up, or still trying to locate trapped passengers?

three coaches of the Bradford train were telescoped. Two passengers were killed, and 13 injured, eight of them seriously, but given the destruction, it might have been a lot worse. The body of one of the dead, slater's labourer Ralph Greenwood Farrand, employed by the L&NWR, was only discovered under the wreckage some hours later as the clear-up was underway. He was to have been married the following day.

As well as incidents caused by equipment failure or human error, 1905 also suffered from some extremes of weather. Hull's Old Paragon Station, for instance, had its roof blown off in a severe storm on 5 January 1905, which also brought torrential rain and some flooding.

The Tunbridge Wells incident which happened on 11 March was officially described as an 'error' while postcards of the event rather coyly described it as a 'mishap when a locomotive ran into a turntable pit'

Another card from Fred Spalding. Given the smoke, still issuing from the wreckage, this may have been taken relatively quickly after the crash.

Lankester & Co. of Tunbridge Wells produced a series of cards of the 'mishap' at Tunbridge Wells and the subsequent recovery of the locomotive. As can be seen from these cards, part of the turntable pit had to be dismantled before the locomotive – a Stroudley Class C1 0-6-0 No.425 – could be dragged out.

There were, of course, no hard and fast definitions to distinguish between one type of incident on the railways and another, so the choice of language used to describe those incidents is fascinating – just how does the writer – and indeed the reader – differentiate between a 'disaster', a 'derailment', a 'collision', an 'accident', or a 'mishap'? Perhaps, in Edwardian terminology, there was an understood order of severity which informed such choices, but if so, it was never written down. But whatever the label, postcards sold well.

Mishap to Large Goods Train Engine at Tunbridge Wells Station, March 11th., 1905.

Mishap to Large Goods Train Engine at Tunbridge Wells Station, March 11th., 1905.

1906 – AT LEAST THE WHISKY SURVIVED UNDAMAGED

The railway accidents of 1906 were covered in many dozens of different postcards, but very few of them were printed in colour – making the card of a derailment at Blairgowrie, Perthshire, a rarity. Interestingly, while it obviously attracted sufficient local interest to warrant the publication of this postcard, with its much more expensive production costs, it is notably absent from the lists of accidents available in online railway archives.

On the morning of 19 December 1906, a goods train approaching Blairgowrie from Coupar Angus was derailed at points just outside the town where the local branch line to Blairgowrie left the main line. The 40-wagon train was hauled by one of the CR's Drummond 0-6-0 'Jumbo Goods', No.590, running tender first. The 'Jumbos' were built between

The wreckage of the derailed train just outside Blairgowrie station. By the time the local photographer and journalist D. G. Monair arrived to set up his camera, a relief engine was already on the scene removing some of the waggons.

below: One of the many other incidents that year, this card shows the wreckage after the derailment of the Norwich train at Shippea Hill – south of Littleport between Norwich and Cambridge – on 10 April 1906. Eight passengers were injured. The Board of Trade report was contradictory is listing 'excessive speed' as one of the contributory factors, while also reporting that, luckily, the train was not going very fast. This postcard is one of a series published by William Charles Barber, using images by David Robert Spencely, whose studio was on Main Street in Littleport. Spencely took up photography around 1891, and by the time he photographed this accident, a former Littleport resident, Warner Gothard, had already moved north to Barnsley, Yorkshire, where he would start producing the composite multi-view cards for which he became famous – several of which can be seen elsewhere in this book.

1883 and 1897 and No.590, built at St. Rollox, was one of the last of a class of 244, entering service in September 1897.

The locomotive jumped the points and stopped abruptly, causing the first ten wagons to concertina into it – two of them finishing up across the both tracks, blocking the line completely. The first wagon had been carrying timber, which was strewn across the trackbed. The second – a box wagon – had been full of 'Christmas goods' which were also scattered far and wide.

The local newspaper the *Blairgowrie Advertiser* reported the incident in its issue for Saturday 22 December noting that

> 'the engine, running tender first, led the way off the metals, and ran along the sleepers for a considerable distance until it left them on one side, and sank axle deep in the soft earth.'

A noteworthy survivor of the crash, according to the newspaper, was 'a large jar of whisky with a wicker-work guard' which was found intact by the trackside. It is reassuring to know that even in the face of a potentially serious accident, the *Blairgowrie Advertiser* did not lose sight of the important things in life.

Clearing the line was achieved remarkably quickly with a breakdown gang – sent from Perth – on the scene within a very short period of time, one line being re-opened in the early afternoon in time for the 13.18 train to access the station.

By that time, two relief engines had also removed the 30 undamaged wagons – steam from one of them can be seen beyond the wreckage, so the postcard photographer and publisher – D. G. Monair of Blairgowrie – must have been on the scene within the first couple of hours. Somehow

two relief locomotives managed to haul the tender back on to the tracks, but No.590 itself had to await the arrival of a steam crane from Motherwell which got there that same evening.

Trains were running in and out of Blairgowrie Station again, on time, by early afternoon – a remarkable achievement. Despite the extent of the damage, nobody was injured in the accident and by the following morning little trace of it remained.

In terms of the sheer number of major incidents, 1906 was a bad year even by Edwardian standards, with serious accidents across the railway network, with at least 68 deaths and more than 350 passengers and train crew injured in notifiable collisions and derailments, but from the point of view of photographers and postcard publishers it was a very busy one.

Two of the many postcards published showing scenes at Salisbury station while the wreckage of the two crashed trains was removed. Twenty-eight people died, and while excessive speed was obviously the root cause, no detailed explanation was forthcoming as the crew had died in the collision. The clear-up took several days with wreckage scattered far and wide. Strict speed limits for trains approaching the station, introduced after the accident, are still in place today.

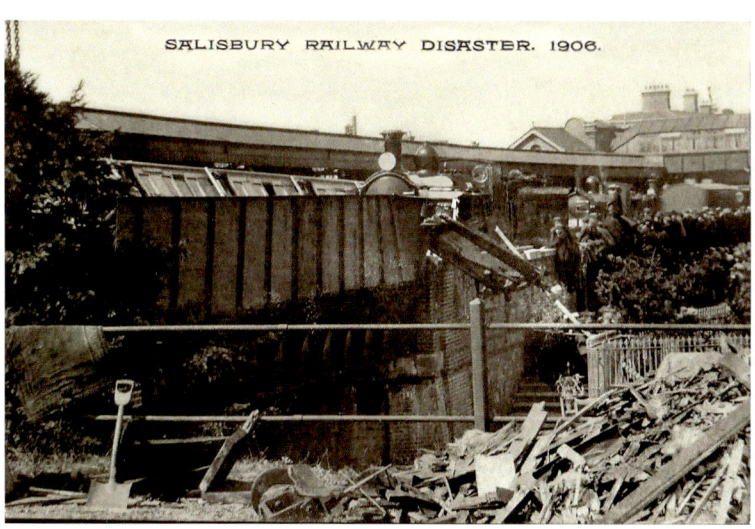

top: Massive crowds of onlookers watch as the wreckage is cleared away from Salisbury Station. Horace Charles Messer's studio was at 29 Castle Street, some distance from the station. Messer had opened his studio in 1897, aged 31 at the time, and would later establish a reputation as an early pioneer of colour photography, using the French 'Autochrome' process. The city of Salisbury reportedly sent a wreath to the funeral of King Edward VII, and Messer photographed it in colour and sent it to King George V as a coronation present.

middle and below: Two postcards from the series produced by F. Futcher of 19 Fisherton Street, Salisbury – a street running just to the east of the station. Most of the wreckage finished up across all four roads just west of Fisherton Street bridge.

Three locomotives were involved in the Salisbury disaster – the L12 class express locomotive, the locomotive pulling the milk train with which the express collided, and a light engine standing at an island platform which was impacted by the wreckage. The official report gives little detail about those other two, except that the milk train was hauled by an 0-6-0 tender engine, and this 1872-built Beyer Peacock goods engine is probably that locomotive.

One of the most heavily photographed of those incidents was the Boat Train disaster at Salisbury station on 1 July 1906. The passengers were, in the whole, wealthy American visitors recently disembarked from the luxury transatlantic liner SS *City of New York*, which had been built at Clydebank by James & George Thomson.

It was, reportedly, not uncommon for limited-stop express trains to run through Salisbury station at night well in excess of the 30mph speed limit – imposed because of the sharp curve approaching eastbound trains had to negotiate.

The L&SWR's boat train, running from Ocean Quay Station at Stonehouse Pool near Devonport to London Waterloo was being hauled by one of the railway's new L12 class of 4-4-0 locomotives No.421, designed by Dugald Drummond and only introduced in August 1905. The engine is said to have had an especially high centre of gravity, making it liable to rock when cornering at speed. Added to that, the driver that night had no prior experience of the route, and was said to have approached the curve at approaching 70mph, more than twice the permitted maximum. A disaster was inevitable. Twenty-four of the 43 passengers and the express train's driver and fireman lost their lives, seven were injured, along with the guard and two waiters in the restaurant car.

In Lincolnshire on 19 September 1906, a Great Northern Railway (GNR) mail and sleeper train from London Kings Cross, bound for Edinburgh Waverley, hauled by Ivatt C1 class 'Atlantic' 4-4-2 No 276 failed to stop at Grantham station as scheduled. The train was derailed, killing 14 passengers and crew. The accident was never explained. The points, on a curve at the end of the platform, had already been set to receive a freight train arriving on the branch line from Nottingham. Two signals, set to caution and danger respectively, had been ignored

right: The wreckage of the express train at Grantham being removed by a Cowans Sheldon travelling crane in the days following the disaster.

middle: Every railway accident drew large crowds of onlookers – today they would probably all have their phones out!

bottom: The wreckage of the express train derailed at Grantham became the subject of several series of locally-produced postcards.

opposite page top: As poignant – and as surprising a subject for a postcard – as the Tay Bridge ticket stubs illustrated on page 22, an un-named postcard photographer has gathered together some of the charred remains of some of the mail retrieved from the wreck site.

opposite page bottom: The wreckage of the express train derailed at Grantham became the subject of several series of locally-produced postcards. Here, the wreck site is being guarded by police.

The Terrible Railway Disaster at Grantham.—Sept. 19th, 1906.

The Terrible Railway Disaster at Grantham.—Sept. 19th, 1906.
Showing the Scattered Mails.

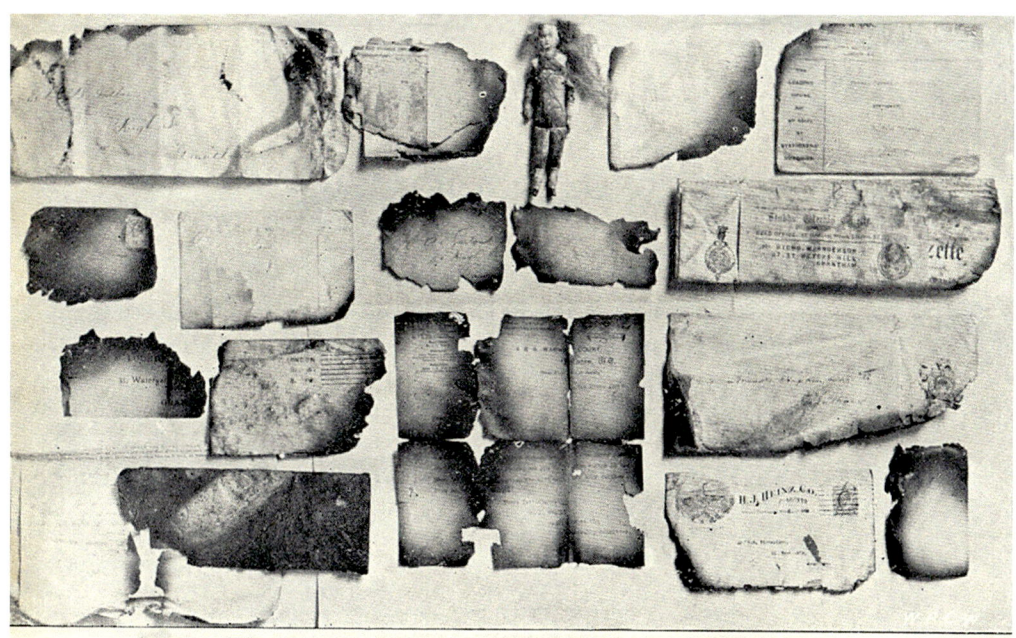

The Terrible Railway Accident at Grantham, on September 19th, 1906.
Fragments of Burnt Letters, &c., delivered through the Post.

by the express. The locomotive itself seems to have been able to negotiate the curve, but the long wheelbase tender jumped the track. The official report acknowledged – 'The only two men who could have given direct evidence as to why the train failed to stop at Grantham, viz... the driver and firemen, were both killed' – leaving the enquiry unable to reach any firm conclusion as to what caused the disaster. Was it human error or equipment failure, or both?

Another high-speed crash had occurred in on 6 April, but luckily with a much lower human cost – just one boy died. It was reported in *The Greenock Telegraph* the following day

'A serious railway accident occurred about nine o'clock last night on the Caledonian main line between Kirtle bridge and Ecclefechan. The train, which was the 2.10 express from London to Glasgow, was travelling at nearly seventy miles an hour, when it dashed

At least three different photographers attended the scene of the Kirtlebridge disaster. Frederick William Tassell of Carlisle was in business as a photographer from the early years of the 20th century, producing portraits in his studio, while also developing a successful postcard publishing business.

Local man, John Murray of Annan, was one of the first photographers on the scene, and his postcards subsequently sold widely. Looking at the extent of the wreckage, it seems remarkable that only one died – a boy of 14 – and 12 passengers and five crew were injured, including the driver and fireman of the express who were very badly burned.

The wreckage of the train at Kirtlebridge inevitably drew crowds of onlookers who were able to roam around the crash site – public health and safety considerations were still decades in the future. The extensive damage to the track resulted in 'about 139 yards of the up line and 117 yards of the down line completely destroyed' according to the official report, with more than 3,000 chairs and 300 sleepers having to be replaced.

into a goods train which had become derailed through a broken axle. The permanent way was torn up for nearly a mile, and both lines completely blocked as a result of the accident. The engine was overturned, and lay on its side on the metals, while the first and second carriages also lay across the rails, making all traffic impossible. The company, in order to expedite other traffic as far as possible, sent all trains, round by Dumfries, on the G&SWR line.'

It is easy to say that the majority of the accidents which occurred during the period of this book should never have happened – but they did keep happening, repeatedly. A notable example was the collision which took place on the NER on 26 November at Ulleskelf Station in Yorkshire. The Board of Trade report recorded that

'In this case, whilst an up empty coal train from York to Gascoigne Wood, consisting of an engine, tender, 60 wagons and a brake van, was standing at Ulleskelf Station, its rear end was run into by the 7p.m. up express train from York to Leeds, consisting of an engine, tender, and four vehicles. The speed of the passenger train at the time of the collision was probably about 40 miles an hour, and the shock was a severe one. The engine was thrown over on to its side, and both it and the tender were severely damaged;

The damage to the signal box, and the wreckage of the two trains after the 7pm express passenger train en route from York to Leeds ran into the back of a stationary goods train at Ulleskelf Station.

The impact caused massive damage to NER 4-4-0 express locomotive No.85, toppling both locomotive and tender, killings its driver and fireman instantly. Two postcards showing both sides of the locomotive suggest that much of the damage was caused by it falling over – while one side is seriously damaged, the other is remarkably unscathed. Two coaches were derailed and eight passengers were injured. In fog and poor visibility, the train had passed and ignored a danger signal. The official enquiry held the dead crew culpable.

the two leading vehicles of the train were derailed, but were only slightly damaged; the two rear vehicles were not derailed and were not injured at all. The brake van and four waggons of the coal train were completely destroyed, whilst three others were seriously damaged. The driver and fireman of the passenger train were both killed instantly, whilst the guard and seven passengers were slightly injured. The guard of the coal train was fortunately not in his brake van at the time, so neither he nor any other of the staff of that train were injured.'

The shock wave and flying debris from the collision caused extensive damage to the signal box. The official enquiry concluded that the crew of the express train were culpable – although as they were dead, they were in no position to disagree, and the facts suggested negligence. The train had been travelling at excessive speed, given that it was foggy, and had missed at least one signal set to danger. The signals two miles north of Ulleskelf Station, and those closest – just over 100 years north of the station – had both been set to danger as neither signalman had received the 'train out of section' call relating to the previous train in order to permit them to be altered. Further up the line, at Bolton Percy, the train had passed three signals at danger. It was later reported that the telegraph cables were broken, so such a signal, even had it been goiven, would never have been reach those signal boxes.

This was a very busy line, and the official report suggested that the fog was, in fact, very thin, and that the real reason why danger signals might have been obscured was residual smoke hanging in the air from two trains which had passed just minutes before. The report made a suggestion which would take many years to adopt.

'This accident, like several previous ones, points to the desirability of the provision of some reliable mechanical contrivance to notify a driver that he is running past a signal. Several railway companies have been, and are, at work on this problem, and a large number of patents have been taken out by inventors, who claim to have solved it. The North-Eastern Railway Company has itself for some years past been experimenting with an apparatus designed for the purpose by one of their officials, and it is at the present time under trial on some of their lines

In the opening chapter of this book, mention was made of the first man reported for being drunk in charge of a train – where luckily nobody had been injured – but a much more serious incident of a driver under the influence of alcohol was determined to be the cause of a major

Multiple factors led to the Eliot Junction disaster, a major one of which was that due to the severity of the weather, a decision had been made to adopt single line working through the station, but that fact had not been communicated to railway staff. It finally stopped snowing at some point in the night of December 28/29 1906, so by the morning the task of clearing up the wreckage could begin.

accident at Eliot Junction between Arbroath and Carnoustie in Scotland as darkness was falling at 3.30pm on 28 December 1906. Twenty-two died, and 24 were injured. An express train, running tender first and at excessive speed in a blizzard, ran into the rear of a local train standing at the platform. The driver of the express had been instructed to 'drive with caution' as there were issues with the signals in the bad weather, but apparently had ignored that instruction. Driver error and excessive speed were cited as the primary causes, with 'driver intoxication' as a secondary cause, although the driver, Gourlay, who survived the impact, insisted he had drunk a tumbler of brandy *after* the collision, not before.

The Eliot Junction disaster was the final disaster in a truly disastrous year, from which railway companies across the country needed to learn many important safety lessons. Several subsequent Board of Trade reports commented critically on the limited view afforded to the crews of many classes of locomotive when running tender first in bad weather.

1907 – PULLING THE WRONG LEVER

By comparison with 1906, 1907 might have been considered a good year for railway safety. There were only 40 accidents considered serious enough to be reported, resulting in a figure of more than 400 injuries to passengers and train crew, and 31 fatalities.

One of the earliest accidents of the year occurred on 16 January when the 6.30 p.m. passenger train from Westbury in Wiltshire to London Paddington, via Chippenham and Swindon, collided with a goods train on its way from Swindon to Plymouth after the driver failed to stop at the signals at Thingley Junction near Chippenham. There were 12 people injured, including the crews of both trains who were badly burned, but luckily no fatalities. The locomotives were both so badly damaged that they were cut up at the accident site.

The train crash at Ebbw Junction on 28 September 1907 was unusual in that it was caused by a signalman pulling the wrong lever. He only realised his error after the collision between a heavy goods train and a high-speed passenger train had taken place. He had pulled No.6 lever, the 'down starting signal', in his frame rather than No.7 which would have cleared the goods train into a passing loop.

below: The engines involved in the Chippenham crash were a River Class 2–4–0 No.70, and Dean Goods 0-6-0 No.2448 – seen here. Both had been designed by William Dean and built at Swindon in the 1890s.

G.W. Railway, Accident at Thingley Junction, near Chippenham Jan. 16th, 1907.
The Goods Engine overturned and fired off

The Shrewsbury crash and the clear-up afterwards were the subjects of extensive newspaper coverage and several series of postcards – many of them variations on the same dramatic scene of the wreckage, their variations offering a narrative on the aftermath. The majority of the postcards, produced by local photographers and printers, were produced very quickly and many were therefore of quite low quality They were, however, on sale within days of the accident. The George Whale-designed 4-6-0 'Experiment Class' locomotive – seen lying on its side in the middle one of these cards was a derivative of the company's earlier 'Precursor' Class. It had slightly smaller driving wheels than the 'Precursor', reportedly offering greater traction. A total of 105 were built at the L&NWR's Crewe Works between 1905 and 1910.

opposite page top: Just four days after the accident, *The Illustrated London News* devoted a page of its issue for 19 October, attempting to explain what had caused the crash. Several of the illustrations were also available on public sale as postcards.

opposite page bottom: This postcard shows the plaque unveiled in 1908 at Shrewsbury Station to mark the deaths of three Post Office workers in the recently introduced travelling post office coach which was part of the express train had which crashed at Shrewsbury Station in October 1907.

A collision was inevitable. The six-coach passenger train was being hauled by a Swndon-built GWR 'Bulldog Class' locomotive 4-4-0 No.3728, brought into service just the previous year. Although badly damaged, it was rebuilt, and continued in service until 1949.

Every disaster has its own story, but the year's worst – which aroused a great deal of controversy – occurred on 15 October outside Shrewsbury Station which was jointly managed by the L&NWR and the GWR. The speeding train had passed signals set at danger and derailed when it reached the points on a complex junction. That single accident accounted for 18 of the 31 fatalities which were reported during the year.

The train – a combined passenger and mail express on its way from Manchester to Bristol and the south west – was hauled by a George Whale-designed London & North Western Railway 'Experiment Class' 4-6-0 locomotive No.2052, one of a class of 105 built between 1905 and 1910.

The train, which left Crewe eight minutes late that night – at 01.28 – was a composite of connecting services from Glasgow and Manchester, and its route from Shrewsbury would have taken it down GWR tracks to Bristol and beyond.

Seven of the passenger coaches were six- or eight-wheeled L&NWR bogied stock and three were six-wheeled GWR stock. Two eight-wheelers were described in the Board of Trade enquiry as 'West Coast Joint Stock'. There was also a Caledonian four-wheeled covered truck and an L&NWR fish van. The accident was reported in both the local and national press, and no lesser publication than *The Illustrated London News* devoted a page to it.

David Lloyd George, then President of the Board of Trade, attended the subsequent inquest, and while the outcome was inconclusive, the enquiry declared that the probable cause was the driver falling asleep as the train accelerated down the slope to Shrewsbury, probably travelling at a speed in excess of 60 miles per hour and derailing on the sharp curve with catastrophic effect – a highly improbable outcome. The enquiry

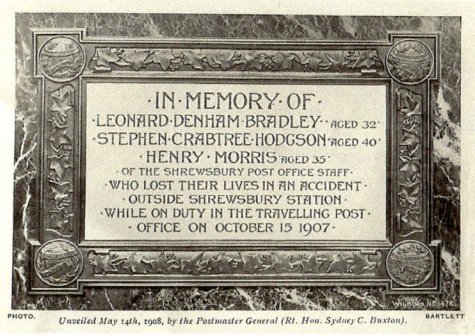

Another of the many postcards of the Shrewsbury crash which were based on photographs taken on the day of the incident and published within just a few days. This was likely taken the morning after the crash.

never fully justified that conclusion and time-served drivers did not believe such a thing to be possible.

While nobody disputed the speed, examination of the wreckage showed that the driver had, in fact, attempted to reverse the locomotive just before the derailment, offering the alternative theory that, despite being virtually new, the locomotive's brakes had inexplicably failed. Had the vacuum brakes on the coaches also failed – or had they been intentionally disabled? The locomotive had actually stopped relatively quickly, but several of the coaches were crushed; others catapulted 200 yards from the rest of the wreckage.

In addition to receiving national press coverage the disaster even inspired poetry, and verses about it were printed in the *Shrewsbury Chronicle*. Although published anonymously, the verses are said to have been written by a 26-year-old local woman, Mary Meredith, whose brother had sent them to the newspaper without telling her – although some sources dispute that, citing one George Creswell as an alternative possible author. Mary Meredith would later gain fame as a poet and successful novelist under her married name of Mary Webb. Although unattributed, this is said to have been her first published work. It included the lines

> Above cold faces that so lately smiled.
> Nigh thirty souls, from this dream scene ascending.
> Before God's throne have reached their journey's ending.
> Their judgment day came swiftly, in the night.
> Through utter tribulation.
> E'en now the angels wipe their tears away,
> Bring them to heaven and comfort them today.

The death toll was, in fact, 18 – far short of the 30 in Meredith's poem – but there were also 61 injured, 30 of them seriously. The dead included two guards, three workers in the travelling sorting office – a service which had been pioneered by the L&MR in 1830 – and 11 passengers.

With both driver and fireman dead, their own account of what actually happened that night would never be heard. However, many railwaymen and their legal representatives vehemently disputed the official findings, demanding, for the sake of the bereaved families, that the stigma of negligence be removed from the dead crew. It never was, and in the eyes of many the Shrewsbury crash remains one of a relatively small number of accidents which have never been satisfactorily explained. In the published accounts from both railway employees and eye-witnesses, a graphic picture emerges of the train crew knowing an accident was about to happen, but being powerless to avoid it.

below left: The damaged coaches after the Taunton collision on 30 April 1907. The metal underframes were undamaged, but the collision ripped out part of the sides of the wooden coach bodies. (*Private Collection*)

bottom: Crowds pose for the postcard photographer in front of the damaged coaches near the Taunton East Junction Signal Box on 30 April.

above: The Ebbw Junction accident near Newport left the goods train driver dead and 15 injured on the passenger train. The GWR 4-4-0 tender engine, No.3728, had been travelling at speed when the collision occurred. Despite the apparent damage, the locomotive was rebuilt, returned to service, and not scrapped until 1949. The photographer, William L. Ballard, had his studio at 1 Stow Hill, Newport, at the time this picture was taken. He later moved to 122a Chepstow Rd.

That was also the case when a collision occurred on the GWR, at Taunton Station in Somerset, on 30 April 1907. Seven passengers and one 'servant of the Company' were originally listed as injured, some seriously, but in July, one of those victims subsequently died of his injuries. According to the official report, the train

> 'consisted of a four-wheels-coupled side tank engine, running chimney first, and three four-wheeled and one six-wheeled coaches. It was fitted throughout with the continuous brake, which is said to have been in good order. The goods train at the time of the collision consisted of a six-wheels-coupled engine, a six-wheeled tender, and 36 waggons and a van. The goods engine was derailed, and both engines and four passenger carriages were badly damaged. The injury to the permanent way was slight.'

The locomotive at the head of the passenger train was a GWR 0-4-0ST, No.537 designed either by William Dean or James Holden, and the goods train was hauled by 0-6-0 tender locomotive No.2432 – a 'Dean Goods', one of a batch of 16 which had been built at Swindon in 1893. The Dean Goods was the reliable primary workhorse for Great Western freight traffic at the time, with 280 being built between 1883 and 1899.

But it is when the report cites the testimony of the driver of the goods train, that the horror of the event unfolds. After shunting a mobile crane into a siding, the driver stated that

'I then got a signal from the guard to steam ahead again, which I obeyed. As I was doing this, I turned round to look ahead, and I saw the steam of the other train approaching Taunton. At first I thought that the train was going on to the down avoiding line, but as the engine of it reached the signal-box, and the steam cleared away, I saw that the signal was lowered for the down main line. My engine was then moving forward. I at once realized that the train would collide with mine. I immediately reversed my engine and gave steam, but was unable to stop in time, and the engine of the train collided with my engine and derailed it.

A crucial contradiction to the signalman's evidence was the driver's assertion – backed up by his colleague – that when he looked up again 'the signals had been set to danger. They were put to danger immediately after the collision.' The enquiry concluded that 'The collision was due to a blunder on the part of signalman Robert Holcombe in the East Junction signal-box', but for the crews of both trains – realising they were about to be involved in a potentially serious collision and being unable to do anything to avoid it – it must have been traumatic.

Eight other accidents resulted in loss of life, the first being at Alnmouth in Northumberland on 14 January when an NER train was derailed and rolled down an embankment. Its cause remains unknown.

below: The overturned locomotive after the Waleswood collision between a partially-derailed goods train and a passenger train, on 16 July 1907. Remarkably, the locomotive crew survived with only minor injuries.

Forty-six passengers were injured on 26 March when buckled rails caused the 10.52am down express from Leeds to Newcastle to derail between Heworth signal-box and Felling Station. The enquiry noted that 'The whole train was derailed with the exception of the last two vehicles, which were partially so. The engine fell over to the left against the south side of the cutting, and the two leading vehicles fell over on to their sides, foul of the up main and adjoining goods lines.' Two of the injured subsequently died of their injuries, and of the others, eight were seriously hurt. The photographer and publisher of the top image is unknown, but the middle and bottom images were photographed and published by G. Hastings of 27 Ridley Place, Newcastle.

Publishers Gale and Polden produced a series of cards in January 1907 of the derailment of a L&SWR Adams T-1 Class 0-4-4T No. 65 near Camberley. The *Pall Mall Gazette* reported

'A train of empty passenger coaches met with a mishap early this morning, shortly after leaving Camberley for Aldershot, on the L. and S.W, Railway. It appears that when at the points dividing the main down line and a short set of rails, the train by some means swerved on to the latter set of metals and collided with an obstruction. The locomotive was hurled, tender first, down an embankment, but the carriages did not leave the rails. The driver, stoker, and guard, all Guildford men, escaped without serious injury. The driver and stoker remained at their post, and when the collision occurred immediately proceeded to bank down the fire of the engine.'

The final fatal accident of the year was at West Hampstead on 26 October when a Metropolitan Railway electric train, running in thick fog, ran into an identical 6-car unit standing at the platform, killing three passengers and injuring 26.

So heavy was the collision that the driving car of the moving train destroyed the first 36 feet of the rear driving car of the other train. Blame was apportioned between the signalman and the train crews for failure to follow a number of company rules, emphasising the signalman's major responsibility.

below: A group of schoolboys pose in front of the L&SWR locomotive at Camberley. The locomotive, designed by William Adam and built in late December 1888, was repaired and returned to service, not being withdrawn until September 1934. It was cut up at Eastleigh in January 1936.

bottom: The schoolboys returned to the scene to watch the retrieval of the locomotive. A second locomotive and a steam crane can be seen positioned at the top of the embankment, ready to haul the tank engine back up the slope.

1908 – 'GOOD GOD! HE WILL BE IN TO THE COAL TRAIN!'

below: Warner Gothard of Barnsley's photo-composite postcards of the Woodhouse Junction disaster included portraits of the dead men – something which became a feature of these cards – and the three wrecked locomotives. (*Mark Fynn / www.warnergothard.com*)

Reading Board of Trade Reports on accidents in 1908 might suggest that while slightly more people were injured than the previous year – 256 as opposed to 248 – there were just eight fatalities. That could hardly be further from the truth.

Two of those deaths occurred on 29 February at Woodhouse Junction near Sheffield, when an 'Emigrant Train', running from Liverpool to Grimsby, collided with a coal train, killing both of the coal train's crew. The term 'Emigrant train' – a term more commonly used in the USA – referred to special trains carrying newly-arrived foreign passengers to their final destinations.

The driver of a passing fish train had predicted the outcome and gave evidence to the official enquiry:

above: Great Central Railway No.852 lying on its side after the Woodhouse Junction collision. The modified Pollitt class D6 4-4-0 was designed by John G. Robinson GCR's s Chief Mechanical Engineer.

'The emigrant train appeared, from what I could see, to be going at a speed of about 25 miles an hour. I was astonished to see the emigrant train, as I knew that the coal train was standing on the up line at the East Junction.... ...I then tried to get the gauge lamp to give the driver of the emigrant train a red light, but I slipped on the footplate, and before I could recover myself, it had passed... ...When I first saw the emigrant train, I said to my mate, "Good God! He will be into the coal train".'

In his evidence he alluded to the awful weather conditions – it was snowing heavily at the time – and the difficulties he had personally experienced that day in seeing and reading the signals. Unusually, due to conflicting evidence, the Board of Trade Inspector's report was unable to reach any firm conclusion as to what had led directly to the accident, concluding:

'The responsibility for this accident rests either on signalman Stokes or on driver Howell and Driver Borland, and the question as to which is to blame hinges entirely on the position of the station signals. The evidence on this point given by one signalman is in direct contradiction to that given by the two drivers; the three men are, however, all interested parties, and unfortunately there is no direct evidence available to corroborate or disprove the statements made on either side.... all that can be said is that the collision was undoubtedly due to a personal error, either on the part of the signalman or on the part of the two drivers.'

One accident where there was no doubt about who was to blame occurred at an unmarked crossing near Northwich Station in Cheshire on 5 November 1908. A branch line used to carry salt from the mine at Barons Quay to Northwich crossed the highway and, in the days before level crossings, a man with a red flag would walk in front of the train as it crossed the road, and vehicles were required to give way.

The salt train was travelling in reverse with the locomotive pushing its wagons, preceded by the man with his flag. A chauffeur-driven car approached the crossing at the same time as the train, the driver ignoring the flag, and not stopping.

As the car was part way across, it was struck by the leading wagon of the train, destroying it, and killing Mrs. Annie Le Neve-Foster of Wilmslow. The driver and another passenger were injured, but survived. The incident is significant, as one of the earliest – if not *the* earliest – occasion in which a motorist was killed by a train. Fifty other people died on railway crossings that year.

In case the reader might think that greasy rails is a modern excuse for railway disruption, it was cited as one of the reasons for a train on the Liverpool Overhead Railway colliding with the buffers at Seaforth Sands Station on 21 December. The primary causes – as with so many accidents – were excessive speed and driver negligence, with the driver realising too late that he should have been moving much more slowly as he approached the station. He applied the brakes hard, and the train skidded for over 100 yards before striking the buffers. A recently qualified electric train driver, this was his first day in sole charge of a train.

In 1909, an astonishing report, titled '*General Report to the Board of Trade upon the Accidents that have occurred on the Railway of the United Kingdom during the year 1908*', was published and, not surprisingly, its conclusions made headlines in most of the country's leading newspapers. It was shocking reading, concluding that over 1,000 people had died on the railways during the year, and nearly 8,000 others were injured. A very different picture from the deaths and injuries in the year's widely reported – and photographed – train crashes.

Of those fatalities, 479 died by trespassing on to the tracks, either accidentally or intending to commit suicide. More than 100 passengers died on trains for whatever reason, of which only eight died in crashes. Railway workers accounted for almost 400 of the deaths, while the causes of the other deaths and injuries were not expanded upon.

Alarmingly, the report concluded that 1908 was not unusual, when compared with the figures for previous years.

1909 – 'NOT A SUITABLE CLASS OF ENGINE FOR RUNNING AT VERY HIGH SPEEDS'

The above heading is taken from the official report into the derailment which occurred at Friezland Station on 10 August 1909 when a train comprising an 0-6-2 tank engine and three coaches jumped the tracks while attempting to negotiate a severe curve at excessive speed. The official report was quite damning:

'The type of engine which was drawing this train, viz., a tank engine with six coupled wheels leading and a pair of radial axle trailing wheels is not a suitable class of engine for running at very high speeds; its wheels are of comparatively small diagonal (5 feet $2^{1}/_{2}$ inches) entailing fast revolution and consequent rapid reciprocating action, while the length (15 feet 6 inches) of the fixed wheel base of its six leading wheels, none of the axles of which are capable of any adjustment on reaching a curve, renders it unsuitable for running round curves at a high rate of speed. That this point is recognised by locomotive engineers is clear from the fact that practically all engines recently designed for use with

For his photo-composite card published a few days after the accident at Friezeland Station, Warner Gothard described the location as being both 'nr Saddleworth' and 'Friezland near Stalybridge'. Both driver and fireman were killed in the derailment and 13 of the 18 passengers received minor injuries. Known as a 'Webb Coal Tank' one example of this L&NWR workhorse survives in preservation. The station was closed in 1917. The Francis Webb-designed 0-6-2T locomotive No.1608 damaged in the derailment was one of a total of 300 built at Crewe between 1881 and 1897. (courtesy of Mark Fynn / www.warnergothard.com)

Despite this postcard of locomotive No.1608 being captioned as 'Greenfield', this is from the same incident illustrated on the previous page – Friezland Station, between Uppermill and Stalybridge on the Huddersfield to Manchester line. (*Private Collection*)

trains running at very high speed are fitted with a radial axle or a bogie in front of their coupled wheels, this radial axle or bogie acting as a pathfinder and thereby assisting the coupled wheels in rear of it to take the curve.'

The accident was the subject of at least two postcards, – the image of the damaged locomotive was captioned as being at 'Greenfield', while Warner Gothard's photo-composite cards said it was 'near Saddleworth'. Neither explicitly said that it happened at Friezland.

Excessive speed and poor rolling stock stability were cited as the primary causes of the accident, in which two died and 14 were injured. The inspector's observation was long overdue, as several earlier accident reports had contained similar concerns about excessive cornering speed

middle: The scale of the widespread wreckage at Sharnbrook offered some dramatic images to postcard photographers. Some, like this, were original photographic prints produced in relatively small numbers. At that time it was possible to buy boxes of photographic paper with the the graphics of a postcard pre-printed on the back. (*Private Collection*)

above: Warner Gothard marked the Sharnbrook disaster with a composite card using two images taken by Spencer Percival of Kettering who, unusually for Gothard, is credited on the card. As was the case with many of Warner Gothard's photo-montage cards, portraits of those who lost their lives featured prominently. (*Mark Fynn / www.warnergothard.com*)

left: Another short-run, postcard, this one also describes the event as 'The Railway Smash' at Sharnbrook. (*Private Collection*)

with locomotives designed for low speed running. It was, however, not the last such incident.

On 21 January, 1909, there were actually three accidents on the same day – two on the L&YR at Fazakerley and Marsh Lane, both near Liverpool, and one on the NBR at Glasgow Queen Street. Thankfully none of them either involved fatalities or attracted photographers. In the case of the Marsh Lane collision, on the same electric line as the 1905 Hall Road, Blundellsands, disaster, thick fog would have made

above: The Tonbridge Junction collision was blamed on errors by the driver and guard on one of the trains, but other factors played their part. (*Mark Fynn / www.warnergothard.com*)

photography impossible. Whereas at Hall Road, the resulting fire was quickly contained, the Marsh Lane disaster saw the fire spread very quickly through the wooden-bodied train. Luckily, there were very few passengers on board and all escaped, although 13 were injured.

One of the year's most-photographed accidents occurred on 4 February, on the Midland Railway at Sharnbrook near Bedford. The extensive devastation after a catastrophic signalling error, quickly admitted by the signalman, caused a head-on collision between two goods trains – in which both driver and fireman of one of the trains died – brought several postcard photographers to the scene, including the splendidly-named Spencer Perceval – named after the assassinated Prime Minister, no doubt – whose images appeared on one of Warner Gothard's photo-composite cards.

Major A. J. Pringle, in his Board of Trade report once again used his favoured terminology writing that the Manchester to London train was 'horsed by a four-wheels-coupled engine' whereas the Bedford to Birmingham train was 'drawn by a six-wheels-coupled good engine'. He had also used of the term 'horsed' in his report on the Cudworth accident near Barnsley in 1905.

In early March there was another serious collision, this time at Tonbridge Junction on the South Eastern & Chatham Railway, involving the 09.05 Continental Mail Express from London Cannon Street to Dover Harbour, and the 08.30 stopping train from Charing Cross to

The derailment on 20 June of a GWR express train from Plymouth, was caused by excessive speed – 55-60 mph instead of 15 mph – while crossing over slip points on a section of temporary 'single-line working'. The train came off the tracks between Highbridge and Bridgwater, and the official report cited six serious breaches of the rules for working over such temporary restrictions.

Dover Town – which were timetabled to reach Tonbridge five minutes apart – and this time blame was attributed to the driver and guard on one of the trains. But there was a complicating factor which underlines the differences in the social protocols between then and now.

In addition to the two trains involved in the accident, and all the other regularly timetabled trains on the line, the Royal Train carrying King Edward VII was scheduled to run through Tonbridge Station shortly after the two Dover-bound trains. The two Dover trains were issued with special instructions to make sure they ran to timetable – thus ensuring they did not inconvenience His Majesty in any way – and to underline that requirement, inspectors were riding on the footplates alongside the rostered crews. Both, however, left London late and arrived at Tonbridge together.

The driver and inspector on the Dover Town train were both killed, and the blame was largely put on the driver of the Dover Harbour driver for allegedly mis-reading a signal. He told the enquiry that he had felt under increased stress with the inspector on the footplate. Three people rather than two in a relatively confined space would certainly have restricted their movement The Board of Trade Inspector's language in the report was clearly prejudicial to Driver Moore, reading

> 'His record is not a very good one. There are several entries against him for over-running platforms and signals at danger. There are five such cases in the last five years.'

The underlying message is clear. However, the lines at Tonbridge remained blocked for some time, and, inevitably, the King's train was delayed.

1910 – 'WILL YOU KISS ME BEFORE I DIE?'

below & opposite: Bertram and William Batchelder, of 109 George Street, Croydon, trading as Batchelder Brothers, had a series of postcards of the Stoat's Nest derailment on sale within four days. Taken under floodlights these remarkable images were the work of an un-named photographer, working for the Topical Press Agency

When the 3.40 p.m. London, Brighton & South Coast Railway (LB&SCR) express bound for London Victoria left Brighton Station on 29 January 1910 – most likely hauled by one of the company's five recently-introduced 4-4-2 'Atlantic' locomotives, although the official report is not specific about which one – nobody could have foreseen the tragedy which would occur less than an hour later when, at Stoat's Nest Station near Coulsdon, part of the train was derailed with the loss of seven lives. According to the subsequent official reports, this was a popular Saturday afternoon train, returning people to London 'in time

below left: The same two Topical Press photographs used on the postcards – showing third class coach No.1325 being lifted away from the track – were used on the front cover of *The Sketch* on 2 February, just four days after the disaster.

below right: Images from both Topical Press and The Illustrations Bureau appeared on page 189 of *The Illustrated London News.* on 5 February. s

for dinner'. It was made up of the locomotive, nine coaches and a brake van, three of the coaches being heavy Pullman cars – 'Albert Victor', 'Prince' and 'Princess Patricia', weighting 28 tons, 28 tons, and 40 tons respectively, compared with the 23-25 tons of a conventional coach – and a 16-ton brake van immediately behind the tender. 'Albert Victor' and 'Prince' had been built in the USA in 1881 and shipped to Britain in kit form for re-assembly, whereas 'Princess Patricia' had been built in Brighton. Between 'Prince' and 'Princess Patricia' were three third class coaches, and it was the middle one of those, No.1325, which appeared to have suffered a failure in the front bogie which caused it to jump the track, initiating a broken front coupling, separating it from the locomotive, brake van and front three coaches of the train.

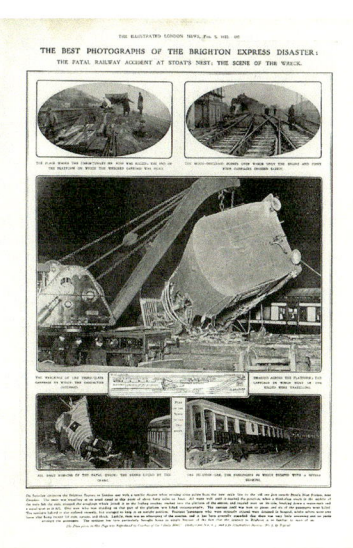

below: The Topical Press Agency's pictures were also used on one of Warner Gothard of Barnsley's photo-composite postcards, now highly prized by collectors. (*Private Collection*)

Breaking that coupling would have required a force in excess of 50 tons. Breaking the offending wheel from its axle on the failed bogie would have required an even greater force, and the LB&SCR would later adopt a policy of regularly testing, during periodic maintenance, just how secure the fit of wheels on axles actually was. The official report noted that

> 'Mr. Wilson Gardner, works manager of the Leeds Wheel and Axle Company, the firm which supplied the wheels of the wrecked coach, said the pressure required to force on the wheels in question was respectively 60 and 80 tons. He could not account in any way for one of the wheels having shifted on the axle.'

The signalman at Stoat's Nest North signal box reported seeing a shower of sparks from the bogie shortly before the train separated, coach No.1325 being thrown in the air and mounting the platform, killing seven people – five women and two men.

Reports are contradictory – some say the women were all passengers on the train while the two men were on the platform, while others report one of the men was also on the train.

The Observer newspaper published an extensive and detailed and heart-breaking account the day after and of the carnage encountered there – later widely syndicated. It noted:

'The first man on the scene was Jack Miller, and he was so overcome by his experience that he was prostrate. He assisted to extricate a young girl who had her chest severely crushed. The girl was just able to speak, and she said to him, "Will you kiss me before I die, so that I may know that somebody loved me?" Jack gave her a kiss and then broke down completely. He walked away and cried.'

She must have been Charlotte Mary Carter, the youngest of the dead, and the daughter of the railway's Brighton-based foreman carriage cleaner. She was about a month short of her 25th birthday. Her body remained unidentified until the following day – one of two victims who lay in the station waiting room until their identities were confirmed. The Board of Trade Inspector would later report at the enquiry – convened the following day – that he had visited the injured in hospital, and had thus recorded evidence from some of the passengers. Their testimony was read out, one significant account being from

'Miss J. Denton, of Battersea, who was on her way home from Brighton, and she described how the carriage she was in swayed passing through the tunnel close to Stoat's Nest. She looked out of the window and saw a dull glow like the reflection of sparks. She was under the impression that the carriage was rolling about before it actually left the rails. Continuing, Miss Denton said "I said to Miss Carter who was travelling with me, "We shall be at Clapham Junction in half an hour. 'Yes;' replied Miss Carter, 'if we ever get there'.

Photographers and reporters were also on the scene very quickly, some even before help arrived.

One of the first was an un-named photographer from the Topical Press Agency which had been set up in 1903 by the well-known press photographer James Barrow Helsby to meet the growing demand for using

below: A small section of *The Observer*'s extensive coverage on 30 January, the day after the crash.

right: The illumination on this Topical Press Agency image of the rescue gives a sense of the power that the incandescent flare lighting and photographers' magnesium flash equipment brought to the scene.

below right: One of the Topical Press Agency images, one by the Illustrations Bureau, and two daylight views by un-named photographers, appeared in *The Sphere* on 10 February

photographs in newspapers rather than the long-established tradition of using line illustrations.

By 1910 Helsby was working out of offices in Red Lion Court off London's Fleet Street and his pictures were widely syndicated within hours of the accident. This was, of course, a time before most newspapers had their own staff photographers, so Topical quickly became the go-to place for news pictures.

Whether it was Helsby himself or one of his colleagues who took the train south to Stoat's Nest with his camera equipment that night is not known – certainly several other photographers did arrive on the scene – but the undertaking marks an important 'first' in the history of photography.

Of all the railway accidents to have taken place in Edwardian Britain, this seems to have been the earliest to be photographed at night under artificial lighting – no mean feat given the scale of the accident scene.

In a long and detailed account from Reuters, published in *The Times* on the Monday after the disaster and later syndicated internationally, the scene was described as 'a strange and sinister spectacle, which the brilliant incandescent flares of the breakdown gang disclosed.'

That powerful lighting would have been acetylene flare lamps fuelled by calcium carbide and water, the most popular of which at the time were 'Carbic' lights manufactured and distributed internationally by C. C. Wakefield & Co. of Cannon Street in London, and they also supplied the calcium carbide in the form of compressed 'Carbic Cake' in different sizes to fit the reservoirs of the many different sizes of lamps.

An entrepreneur with a multi-faceted career, Charles Cheers Wakefield is also credited with improving the performance of engine

below left: Charles Cheers Wakefield patented his 'Carbic' flare lamp in 1905.

below right: An American advertisement for carbic lamps, c.1910

bottom: An acetylene flare jet c.1910. These portable lamps provided several hours of intense light, and in addition to providing emergency lighting at incidents like Stoat's Nest, many were also used – as in this photograph – to illuminate London traffic junctions in times of heavy fog.

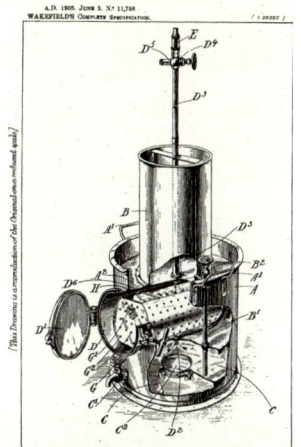

No.41, one of the five Marsh HI Atlantic' 4-4-2 locomotives built between December 1905 and February 1906 operated by the London, Brighton & South Coast Railway. It was an HI which hauled the Brighton to London express which crashed at Stoat's Nest

A Cowans Sheldon 15 ton crane of the type used at Stoat's Nest – this 1912 example awaits restoration at the Whitehead Railway Museum north-east of Carrickfergus. (© *Image courtesy of The Railway Preservation Society of Ireland.*)

oil by adding castor oil – creating the well-known 'Castrol' brand. That report, however, was critical of media activity at the scene, noting that

> 'The only disturbing element was the presence on a hill overlooking the station of some photographers, whose dazzling flashlights hampered the railwaymen in their delicate task.'

Night photography using artificial light was still very much in its infancy in 1910. Early press photographers used large tripod-mounted cameras and either glass plates or large sheets of film, and even in daylight such a combination required quite long exposure times.

Despite the amount of lighting brought in by the rescue teams, high-intensity illumination from primitive open flash units – the light created by exploding magnesium powder – was needed to expose the photographic plates. The flash was triggered after the camera shutter had been opened, creating an eerie double-exposure in some of the pictures before the shutter was closed again. Given that working under such conditions was almost experimental in nature, the quality of the pictures is remarkable.

Photographers from rival photo agency 'The Illustrations Bureau', also arrived that night, but their photographs – some of which were used in The *ILN* – are less striking than those taken by Topical's photographer.

Perhaps surprisingly for 1910, instead of using a photograph on its front cover of its issue for 5 February, The *ILN* chose to illustrate the carnage with a specially created artwork based on the recollection of one of the passengers. Bizarrely, it showed the scene in daylight rather than in the middle of the night. By daylight the wreckage had actually been completely cleared away In addition to the national and international press, *The Sketch*, a society magazine, covered the story just four days later, while *The Sphere* published a detailed illustrated account in its issue for 10 February. The most widely publish image – appearing in *The Sketch*, *The Sphere* and others as well as on postcards, was the dramatic shot of the wrecked coach being craned clear of the line.

The Sphere noted that amongst the earliest rescuers were 12 boy scouts from the 4th Purley Coulsdon Group, known as 'Princess Christian's Own Troop', who turned up complete with stretchers and first aid equipment, and helped injured passengers away from the wreckage and on to the station platforms. Their participation is marked by a Bourne Society 'Blue Plaque' on the site of the station which closed in 1983.

But there was little that the rescuers could do about anyone who might be trapped under the wreckage of the coach until it was lifted clear by two heavy cranes – the first one coming from New Cross, another from Brighton – which arrived around 8pm. The crane seen in the contemporary photographs was built by internationally-renowned crane-maker Cowans Sheldon of Carlisle. Along with the cranes, the railway breakdown crews brought powerful acetylene flare lamps to enable the rescuers to work through the night. Perhaps most surprising is that, throughout the early stages of the rescue, the station remained open, with trains arriving and leaving at the other platforms. By morning, the wreckage had been moved to New Cross for minute examination.

The *Daily Mirror*, in its report on 1 February, chose not to show the wrecked train, but to publish a photograph of two budgies which had been on the train with their owner, Dr Edward Kellett, assuring readers that all three had escaped unhurt.

The official report identified the broken axle as the primary cause, laid no blame on any railwaymen, but advised the LB&SCR to consider adopting enhanced checks of the wheels and axles to minimize the risk of something similar happening in the future.

Whilst the coverage of the Stoat's Nest incident was considerable, the press coverage of the year's other fatal accidents on mainland British railways seems to have been rather low key. Elsewhere on the network, 31 people died in nine fatal accidents, and just over 300 were injured, some seriously.

The worst was late in the year, at Willesden Station on 5 December, when five people died and 147 were injured, as a result of a busy L&NWR

top: In 1910, the tapered bellows camera was still the choice of most professionals. This model, by W. Tylar of Aston, Birmingham, was available in half plate and quarter plate sizes. Did the photographers at Stoat's Nest use such an instrument? ….

above: ….or had they adopted the latest 'Ruby Reflex' camera, manufactured by the Altrincham-based Thornton-Pickard company who had started manufacturing cameras in 1888?

train colliding with a stationary train due to a signalling error. The report made difficult reading

> 'The effects of the collision were disastrous. The stationary train, consisting of 10 bogie carriages and engine, was driven forward about two engine lengths. Fortunately the brakes were off, or matters would have been even worse. The two last coaches were "telescoped", that is to say, the frame of the last coach got below the frame of the coach next in front of it, and was forced under it for about four-fifths of its length, so that nearly the whole of the body of this last coach was swept clean off the frame, and forced against the front end of the engine of the second train. The coach was well filled, and the scene presented to persons on the platform must have been shocking. It is believed that all the persons who were fatally injured were in this coach. The body of the second coach from the rear was badly damaged, especially at the ends, but remained on its frame, and struck the edge of the platform roof, doing some slight injury to it. The bogies of the rear coach remained below it, but were off the rails and out of position; the bogies of the second coach were torn from under it, and were found close together between it and the nest coach in front. The third coach had its rear end damaged and was derailed.'

The frames of one vehicle sliding under another echoed the Hall Road collision at Blundellsands on the Liverpool to Southport line in 1905. In his conclusions, Colonel H. A. Yorke, the Board of Trade Inspector, made some significant recommendations.

> 'The modern steel under-frames in use in this country are only about 9 inches deep, so that a comparatively small amount of vertical movement will permit of one frame getting above the other.
>   It suggests itself to me that it might be possible to modify the designs of the under-frames so as to give a considerably increased depth to the ends of headstocks of them. If, for instance, it were found possible to increase the depth of the headstock by 9 inches, the relative vertical movement between two coaches, necessary to allow one to mount upon the other, would be increased from 9 to 18 inches, which would be an advantage. If the frames could also be made to interlock with each other as soon as they came in contact, the risk of one frame mounting another would be still further reduced. The subject is one to which the attention of the Railway Companies of the United Kingdom might be drawn'.

1911 – 'GOOD GOD! THERE IS A MINERAL ON No.1'

The new year did not start well at Hopkinstown near Pontypridd on the Taff Valley Railway when, for the second time in that line's history, a major disaster caused considerable loss of life. Due to a signalling error on 28 January, a passenger train – the 09:10 from Treherbert to Cardiff – carrying around 100 people, ploughed into a stationary coal train, killing 11 and injuring a further five. The coal train had been stopped at the No.1 down line home signal on instruction from the Rhondda Cutting signal box. It was the third of four notifiable accidents to occur that month, and the first to record a loss of life.

Confusion in the signal boxes was determined to be the root cause, with the signalman, Albert Hutchings, deemed to have broken established rules of 'block working' – the protocols for passing trains from one section of line to another. Realising too late what he had done Hutchings is reported to have shouted 'Good God! There is a mineral on No.1' while trying – too late – to change the signals, hoping to avoid the inevitable collision. He then collapsed.

The Board of Trade Inspector's report was complicated by the fact that the clocks in the signal boxes showed a difference of several

below: One of the postcards showing the aftermath of the Hopkinstown collision, photographer unknown. (*private collection*)

above: The Sphere carried a full-page annotated photograph of the Hopkinstown disaster on the cover of its issue for 28 January.

below right: GCR No. 217 was shunting seven waggons when it was hit by the 'runaway train' near Wombwell, one of a production run of 174 'Class 9J' locomotives built in several batches between 1901 and 1910. The 9J was an 0-6-0 goods engine designed for the railway by John G. Robinson. The runaway train itself was being hauled by recently rebuilt 9J, No.472, which had returned to service the previous month. The wreckage was photographed by local Barnsley photographer and postcard publisher George Washington Irving.

minutes – curiously explained in the inquiry by the fact that the accident had happened just after 09.30, and the signal-box clocks were not synchronised until 10 am each day. 'Railway time' being of paramount importance, one would have expected reliable and accurate timepieces to have been in everyday use in such key locations as signal-boxes. Signalling errors – at the same Rhondda Cutting signal-box – had also been blamed for an even worse disaster 33 years earlier when an empty passenger train was reversed into a busy passenger train, resulting in 13 deaths and more than 100 injured.

The cause of the collision between two goods trains at Wombwell on the Chapeltown Branch of the GCR at Wombwell on 19 December was a combination of the driver losing control of his train, disregarding accepted operational protocols for this line.

This stretch of line had a gradient of 1 in 44, very steep for a heavily laden coal train, and to minimise risk, the rules required the driver of trains descending the gradient to stop at Rockingham South signal box and apply handbrakes to every other waggon before slowly proceeding. There was no question about the locomotive's brakes – it had only returned to service earlier in the month after a major rebuild at the Gorton Works – but every driver knew that the locomotive brakes alone could not contain the train on that descent. To complicate matters, the Rockingham South signal box was closed at night, and the driver was relatively new to the route, so may not even have noticed he was at the designated stopping point. Just why the rules were broken will never be known, as the driver and fireman both died at the scene, but instead

of slowly descding the gradient, the train, without the waggon brakes applied, rapidly increased speed. Instead of about 4mph, by the time it reached Rockingham Hoyland, the next box on the long descent, it was running at 16mph and accelerating, so totally out of control by then that its speed was still increasing. It had reached something approaching 60mph when the crash occurred at Wombwell just three miles further on. As the postcards of the aftermath show, the devastation was considerable.

The official report was highly critical of the night-time closure of the Rockingham South box, while the GCR itself promised to take remedial measures to obviate a similar event happening again. The Inspector, Lieut. Col. P. G. von Donop, R.E., noted that

> 'The Company inform me that with the view of preventing such serious consequences resulting from a train getting out of a driver's control, they are arranging to construct in a suitable position on the down side of Wombwell Junction, a sand drag similar to those in use on the Lancashire and Yorkshire Railway.'

below & bottom: Colonel von Donop's report described the Wombwell accident and the wreckage in great detail – 'In this case as the 12.35a.m. up coal train from Sheffield to Wath Yard, consisting of an engine, tender, 44 loaded waggons, 12 empty waggons and a brake van... ...got out of the control of the driver, and, after passing several signals at danger, came into collision with seven waggons which were being shunted... At the time that the collision occurred the runaway train was travelling at a very high rate of speed, and the damage to the rolling stock was consequently considerable. The engine of the runaway train was derailed and thrown over on its side, and it was then completely covered by coal and the debris of broken waggons. The fireman was killed instantaneously and the driver died before he could be released from the wreckage.'

1912 – 'THE DAMAGED BRIDGE BORE STRIKING TESTIMONY'

below: The remains of 3rd Class Brake No.7236. Most of the train's wooden-bodied coaches were lit by gas, and the ferocity of the collision with the bridge caused burst gas pipes and fires, with tragic consequences.

By all accounts, 1912 appears to have suffered relatively few major disasters on the railways. There were 22 injured at Washwood Heath in January, 86 at London Fenchurch Street in February, and two serious accidents in June – 17 injured at Murton Junction on 19 June and, just two days later four dead and 63 injured at Vauxhall in London.

Thirty were injured at Caledonian Road in London on 4 Sept, but the disaster which made the national headlines was the terrible crash and resulting fire at Ditton Junction on 17 September. The driver and fireman, and 13 passengers died, and the guard and somewhere between 38 and 50 passengers – reports differ as to the exact number – were injured, several of them very seriously. Driver error was cited as the

primary cause, and the official enquiry report opened with a descriptive statement which actually makes the death toll seem remarkably light!

'In this case, as the 5.30 p.m. passenger train from Chester to Liverpool was passing from the fast line to the slow line at Ditton Junction, through the cross-over road at the east end of the station, the engine and carriages were derailed and wrecked with terrible results. Some of the carriages caught fire and were wholly or partially burnt. Fifteen persons, including the driver and fireman, were killed, some of them being burn; and 39 passengers and the guard were injured, the injuries in eight cases being of a serious nature.'

It would have been of only minimal comfort to the families of the deceased to be assured after the event that their loved ones had been killed by the force of the impact, rather than having been burned to death in the destroyed coaches. It did, however, take more than two hours for the gas fires to be extinguished, despite the best efforts of the attending Widnes Fire brigade.

Just how fast the train was going is evidenced by the wreckage of the locomotive which was distorted and

below: L&NWR 'Improved Precedent Class' locomotive No.1529 *Cook* was destroyed as it hit the bridge pier. Both driver and fireman were killed. This Topical Press Agency image was used in several newspapers the day after the Ditton disaster.

bottom: Philip T. Ford of Widnes took a series of images which were published as locally-produced postcards.

right: The clear-up of the wreckage took some considerable time, followed by the complete replacement of over 100 yards of track. (*Private Collection*)

below: The burned-out interior of coach No.7236, another postcard photographed the following day, and published by Philip T. Ford of Widnes, after the fires had been extinguished and the wreckage cooled down.

compressed almost beyond recognition. The train's speed at the crossover, should have been no more than 15 mph, but it was, reportedly, doing about 60mph. But just to blame the driver over-simplifies the cause, and the report noted that afterwards, signalling was changes to make it less confusing to drivers – driver Newton was relatively new to the route –and noted the fact that the L&NWR did not use trackside speed boards to alert drivers as they approached potential hazards.

The disaster also led to renewed recommendations that gas lighting be removed from railway carriages – which had been made quite forcibly

in several previous accident reports – most notably the accident at Hawes Junction the previous year – noting that only two coaches had electric lighting. Railway companies offered conflicting reasons for not implementing those recommendation, most notably claiming electricity was more expensive than gas.

Excessive speed had also been cited as the primary cause, just three months earlier on 21 June, when a train was derailed on a tight curve at Hebden Bridge on the L&YR. Four died and more than 60 were injured.

The speed limit on that curve was 45mph, and the train's speed was estimated to be in excess of 50mph – not much over the limit, but enough to cause the locomotive to jump the track. The report conceded that during recent modifications to the curve, to lessen its severity the decision had been made not to replace a guide rail, and that a driver had no accurate way of monitoring his speed and relied on his experience. The Inspector, Lieut.-Col. E. Druitt, made the obvious observation that:

> 'it would be well for the speed round this and other curves at the end of long gradients to be sometimes recorded by instruments, or by speed recorders placed on the engines, so that drivers could be told when they exceeded the authorised speed, and taught what a speed of 45 miles an hour and other speeds really are, as it must be difficult for them to discriminate between such speeds as 45, 50, and 55 miles an hour, especially on goods roads and on steep gradients.'

Such equipment had, in fact, been available for decades, but had not been widely adopted, and every Brighton-built locomotive had been fitted with a speed indicator before 1910.

below: The wreckage of the train derailed at Hebden Bridge. Bottom left is locomotive No.276, an Aspinall 2-4-2ST tank engine, later deemed to be unsuitable for travelling at high speed.

1913 – 'THERE WAS A BLOCK ON THE LINE AT COLCHESTER'

below: Warner Gothard's photo-composite card commemorating the crash used images of the wreckage taken by Charles A Mather, whose 'Royal Studio' was in Brightlingsea.

When it comes to understatement, that instruction issued to ticket office staff at London Liverpool Street Station was a classic. The 'block' was as the result of a major collision on 12 July which closed Colchester station for some time.

The quote comes from a statement given in Parliament in response to customer complaints about train delays, that statement having included 'testimony' from the ticket clerks on duty:

'Mr. Whipps,—I received an intimation of the blockage at Colchester shortly after 4.0 p.m.. and I was then instructed by Mr. White to inform passengers that there was a block on the line at Colchester, and that there would probably be delay. I carried out these instructions until I left about 9.0 p.m.

above: The wreckage at Colchester Station after the Cromer Express crash on 12 July. This is No.6 of a series of postcards published by Cullingworth & Co of 156 High Street, Colchester.

left: No.5 in Cullingworth's series, this postcard shows the GER's Class S69 locomotive No.1506. A total of 51 of these 4-6-0 locomotives, designed by Stephen Dewar Holden, were built at the company's Stratford Works over a 10-year period between 1911 and 1921. A batch of twenty more were built by William Beardmore & Co in Dalmuir, Glasgow, and the design continued to be built into the LNER era. No.1506 was from the first batch built at Stratford in late 1911. The locomotive was scrapped after the disaster.

Mr. Nenan,—I received instructions at the same time as Mr. Whipps, and both Mr. Prime and myself, who were at the third-class windows, carried out the arrangement. Between 8.0 and 9.0 p.m. Mr. White asked us if we were still advising passengers, and was assured that this was being done. We then made the remark that we were quite hoarse in talking to the passengers. Some took very little notice of the intimation, while others wanted to enter into discussion and asked several questions, which we were unable to answer. There is no doubt whatever about the passengers in the 5.30 p.m. or in any other train being properly advised.'

right and below right: Nos. 3 and 4 from Cullingworth & Co's extensive series of postcards of the wreckage of the Colchester disaster. Cullingworth & Co. had been registered at Stationers' Hall as printers and stationers since 1871. The name of the photographer who took these pictures is not recorded. The juxtaposition of human figures amongst the wreckage give a powerful sense of just how devastating the accident must have been.

So what actually happened? A simple statement that the express from Cromer to London ran into a light engine on the same track overlooks a series of inter-acting errors and rule breaches on the part of the signalmen.

Had the Sykes 'lock and block' equipment been correctly applied – prohibiting the express from entering the section before the light engine had cleared it – such a collision should have been impossible.

Part of the blame was also attributed to the driver of the light engine for failure to follow 'Rule 55' – already cited in a number of the accidents mentioned in this book – which required him to send his fireman to the nearest signal box, whatever the weather conditions and whatever the distance, to alert the signalmen of the locomotive's presence when he brought his engine to a standstill on a running line.

Rule 55 had been brought in specifically to prevent collisions of this sort by ensuring that staff in signal boxes never forgot that there might be a stationery train on the line, and that appropriate signals should be set to either slow down or bring to a standstill any other trains on the line. The signalman should then have slipped a collar or collars over the appropriate levers to remind him that there was a standing train. The Inspector, Lieut.-Col. P. G. von Donop, who had written many such reports, noted that this was the third time in a year that this combination of errors had resulted in a light engine being forgotten about. That collar should not have ben removed until the standing train was known to be 'out of section' and would thus have prevented the signal being altered by accident The driver and firemen of the express, and the guard travelling in the brake van immediately behind the tender were all killed.

below: locomotive's damaged tender, photographer unknown'. This was the image used bottom left in the Gothard composite card illustrated on page 96 (*Private Collection*).

bottom No.12 from an extensive series of postcards by Ernest Morter of 75/75a Military Road, Colchesters. Interestingly, he captioned his cards as a 'train disaster' rather than a 'railway disaster'.

1914 – THE APRIL DAY THE 'FLYING SCOTSMAN' CAME OFF THE RAILS

below: Just four days after the Burntisland collision and derailment, in its issue for 18 April 1914, the illustrated news magazine *The Sphere* carried an extensive account of the disaster, featuring this view of the operation to clear the wreckage.

When Warner Gothard produced his photo-composite postcard to commemorate the railway disaster at Burntisland in Fife on 14 April 1914, he committed a grievous sin in the eyes of many Scottish people – not to mention the NBR. He referred to the train as the 'Flying Scotchman' rather than the 'Flying Scotsman'. And, indeed, the 'Flying Scotsman in those days was a train and not the locomotive which later bore that name. The locomotive 'Flying Scotsman' was not built until 1923. It carried the London & North Eastern Railway number 4472 in its heyday or – as at the time of writing – its British Railways number 60103,

On that fateful day in April 1914, the train was being hauled by an eight-year-old NBR 'Atlantic' 4-4-2 'H Class' locomotive carrying the name 'Auld Reekie'. The NBR favoured the 4-4-2 wheel arrangements as it made it easier to negotiate some of their network's tighter curves, and 20 of these powerful locomotives had been built between 1906 and 1911 – a further two, with modifications, would be built in 1921.

The collision occurred a few minutes before five o'clock in the morning, when the express train collided with a goods train which was being backed out of its way at a crossing point between the up and down lines just outside Burntisland station. The passenger train was on its way

from Edinburgh to Aberdeen, the slow-moving goods train from Carlisle to Dundee. Both trains were running late, and the decision was made to move the goods train off the line to allow the free passage of the express but, due to a signalling error, it all went wrong. No evidence was possible from the express locomotive's crew as in the collision they were thrown from their cab before the locomotive toppled on top of them, crushing both of them to death. The goods train driver, however, gave a full account:

In Major J. W. Pringle's subsequent Board of Trade report, the location of the busy junction was described in detail:

'Burntisland Station, on the Company's main road between Edinburgh and Dundee, is situated 10 miles north of the Forth

below: The Warner Gothard postcard of the Burntisland collision used a stock photograph of the locomotive taken when it was introduced in 1906, the photograph of the crash scene also featured in *The Sphere*, and a view of spectators looking at the wreckage, photographer unknown. (*Private Collection*)

bottom: It is hard to imagine that NBR No.872 'Auld Reekie' – seen here on its side on Burntisland Golf Course after the collision – could be repaired and returned to service, but it was, continuing to haul express trains until it was withdrawn in 1935. (*Private Collection*).

below right: No.12 in a series of postcards of the goods train crash at Andover on 13 October 1914. It was photographed by prolific postcard publisher Fred Wright, whose studio was in Andover's Jewry Street. Wright was best known for his portraits, – especially his many group portraits of soldiers at Tidworth Barracks in Wiltshire. (*Private Collection*)

bottom right: For this card of the goods train collision at Reading on 17 June, Gothard used five photographs. The original prints, probably no bigger than 10x8 inches in size, would have been pasted on to a large board, lettering added, and then the whole montage re-photographed by a postcard-sized camera. Each resulting postcard was an original handmade photographic print and no two cards were identical. (*Private Collection*)

Bridge. It is an important locomotive and traffic centre on account of the Harbour and Docks.'

He went into considerable detail about the timings of the two trains on that fateful day noting that 'There is direct conflict on one, though not the most material point'. He continued:

'It will be seen that the passenger express was 26 minutes late leaving Edinburgh, and had not made up any time when it

passed Burntisland Junction. The Carlisle train was 21 minutes late starting from Dalmeny and 28 minutes behind time at the Junction. The latter is booked to shunt at Burntisland for the express, and is due to arrive at the Junction 9 minutes before the express. On this occasion it was seven minutes in front.'

Those missing two minutes possibly made the difference between the goods train being clear of the cross-over, and it partially blocking the express's path, although Pringle enumerated several signalling errors as the primary cause, noting that:

'For the above reasons I hold that the responsibility for this collision rests with signalman Watt. It is so far to his credit that he frankly admitted the responsibility. He has twelve years' service with the Company and has been a signalman eleven years. He is a life-long total abstainer, and a man of good character.'

Elsewhere, on 18 June, an surprising accident occurred on the Highland Railway (HR) for which nobody could be blamed. Torrential rain caused flooding which totally washed away a 17-year-old granite-built bridge over the Baddengorm Burn at Carrbridge just as a train from Inverness to Perth was passing over it. Five people died. Extreme weather conditions, it would seem, are nothing new.

A photographer from the *Dundee Courier* newspaper took a series ofe photographs of the carriages lying in the Baddengorm Burn at Carrbridge in which five people died and 10 were injured. They were later published as postcards. The torrent of water which was funnelled through a gorge upstream completely swept the bridge away just as the train started to cross over.

1915 – QUINTINSHILL – THE RAILWAY'S DARKEST DAY

Firemen damping down *below:* the last of the fires on the wrecked sleeping cars of the Glasgow-bound train at Quintinshill. The journalistic style of many of the postcards was similar to the type of images starting to appear in the daily newspapers. The official death toll (later modified) was 227 dead and 246 injured.

During the 16 years covered by this book, countless lives were lost as a direct result of railway accidents. The actual figure is unknown and beyond any reliably accurate assessment due to the inadequacy of available records, but one thing that is certain is that approaching a quarter of all those listed as killed in official reports between 1900 and 1915 died on a single day – 22 May 1915 when five trains collided on what is now the West Coast Main Line, near Gretna in the Scottish Borders, causing Britain's worst-ever railway disaster. Two hundred and thirty people died at Quintinshill – passengers and crew – with many hundreds more being seriously injured. Twelve of the deaths were on the 'Scotch Express' sleeper train from London to Glasgow which had left Euston 30 minutes late; two were on the local train from Carlisle, and 216 on a troop train en route south from Larbert in central Scotland, travelling in obsolete wooden-bodied coaches, brought out of storage years after they ought to have been condemned.

In 1915, Board of Trade reports listed 43 rail crash deaths for the whole country *apart from Quintinshill* – the highest since 1906.

1915 – QUINTINSHILL – THE RAILWAY'S DARKEST DAY

Burning Train, Gretna Green Railway Disaster May 22, 1915.

top: One of the first photographs of the disaster shows one of the sleeping carriages ablaze on the Euston to Glasgow express.

middle: The Glasgow-bound express was double-headed, with 'Dunalistair IV' or '140' Class 4-4-0 No.140 acting as pilot engine. In front of the locomotive is the tender from the troop train. The locomotive has actually ridden over the wreckage of the troop train. The second locomotive was No.48, another 'Dunalistair Class'. This type of locomotive was also hauling the troop train – No.121. The local train was hauled by 'Cardean Class' 4-6-0 No.907.

bottom: The aftermath of the disaster, with dead and wounded being extricated and stretchered towards the waiting ambulance train which the Caledonian Railway rushed to the scene.

TERRIBLE TROOP TRAIN DISASTER.
One of the express engines telescoped on top of the wreckage of the troop train. The tender (on the left) has been thrown right over the side of the track.

7th ROYAL SCOTS helping their wounded comrades in the Gretna Green Railway Disaster, May 22nd, 1915

As the caption on this postcard explains, just over 10% of the Royal Scots who were on the troop train were able to turn out for the roll call.

THE RAILWAY DISASTER NEAR CARLISLE.
A roll of the troops was called at 11.30. Fifty-two men of the Royal Scots answered the roll call out of about 500. A large number of the survivors accompanied their wounded comrades to the hospital, and the roll call was in consequence incomplete. The photo shows the calling of the roll.

The disaster happened at a time when photographs were starting to be used in newspapers, and the photographic postcard was at the peak of its popularity. The visual language of telling a story through photographs was becoming increasingly sophisticated. Thus the visual narrative of the photographic postcards produced of the accident was comprehensive.

Ever since the accident, questions have been asked about how such a disaster could have been possible – after all, railways had been improving their safety records, signalling was improving and brakes on locomotives and coaches were reportedly much more efficient than before. But there were significant factors which caused the carnage at Quintinshill – and obsolete wooden-bodied coaches with bottled gas lighting were near the top of the list.

As in so many earlier accidents, the official report into the disaster cited two probable causes in particular – each inextricably linked to the other – and they were 'signalling error' and, once again, 'failure to comply with Rule 55'. The report was never fully accepted by the public, or the families of those involved and, over the years the disaster and its aftermath have sometimes been referred to as the 'Quintinhill Conspiracy', with claims that the report fell far short of telling the full story. It is strongly believed by historians that the actual cause of the accident was much more complicated than the Board of Trade report concluded.

At the time of the incidents – for there were multiple collisions rather than a single one – the trains were under the control and supervision of Quintinshill signal-box which was just a few yards from the crash site. While wartime train movements meant that there was 40% more traffic for the time of day than would have been the case in peacetime – and

TERRIBLE TROOP TRAIN DISASTER.
ONE OF THE TELESCOPED CARRIAGES.

The fragility of the old wooden is only too apparent in this postcard view. It show the partially-destroysed leading coach of the local Caledonian Railway train. Errors in the signal boxes – particularly the signalmen's failure to follow the protocols laid down in 'Rule 55' – were cited as the primary causes, Only two of the deaths were of passengers travelling on this train, but many others were injured.

the incidents also bridged a change-over of signal box crew – the direct line of sight from the signal-box to the junction should have reduced the likelihood of a collision. But life is never that simple. The report began with a simple summary of the salient contributory factors:

'In this case a special troop train from Larbert to the south collided with the 6.10 a.m.* local train from Carlisle to the north, which had been crossed over from the down to the up line opposite Quintinshill Signal-box, and shortly afterwards the wreckage was run into by the 6.5 a.m. express passenger train from Carlisle to the north.'

The asterisk linked to a footnote noted that the 6.05 train from Carlisle was locally known as the 6.17 as that was the time it usually left. Had it left at 6.05am, might there have been a very different outcome – the signal-box crew change-over would have been completed before the troop train arrived? Probably not. That change-over had handed control of the box to James Tinsley, and Tinsley was clearly not well.

So, what did Rule 55 require of the signalmen? It was cited in several accident reports studied during the research for this book and, although quite convoluted, should have been a good and reliable safety feature, relying on the physical application of a 'Lever Collar'. The report concluded:

'When a Train has been shunted on to the opposite Running Line. For each of the operations mentioned above, or in any other case of the Line being blocked, the Signalman must place the

Lever Collar over the handle of the Lever working the Signal which protects the Line upon which the obstruction exists, and so prevent the Signal from being lowered until the Collar is removed.

When a "Lever Collar" has been used for the protection of a Train in accordance with the foregoing, the Signalman must not remove it from the handle of the Lever until he is personally aware that the Train has been shunted clear of the Line on which it had been standing, or he has been informed by the Shunter or Guard that this has been done.

When the Guard, Shunter, or Fireman has satisfied himself, in accordance with the provisions of Rule 55, that his Train has been protected by the use of a Lever Collar or other appliance provided in the Signal-box for this purpose, he may return to his Train.

N.B.-The Lever Collars when not in use must, where practicable, be placed on the spare Levers, but, where this cannot be done, they must be hung up in a convenient place in the Signal-box.'

George Hutchinson, the fireman on the freight train had, as the rule required, gone to the signal-box to check the collar was in place on the lever, but became involved in a conversation about other things, and returned to his train without actually having personally checked that it had been done. It was rumoured that failure to follow Rule 55 by conducting a personal visual confirmation was widespread, but exploring that suggestion was not officially pursued.

While the procedures required of the signalmen were clearly laid out, they failed to follow them to the letter – but it is said that a general 'slackness' in the application of Rule 55 was widespread across the Caledonian Railway and the network as a whole. That has led to a strong case subsequently being made by railway historians that there may have been complicity in a cover-up on the part of the company, and the ramping up of the importance of the part played by the signalmen, to the exclusion of other contributory factors.

So, what went wrong on that fateful Saturday morning? Was it a simple lack of concentration during the change-over, or was the impact of other contributory factors never fully considered during the Board of Trade and subsequent Coroners' Court proceedings?

Was that an unwritten requirement? Were the signalmen 'sacrificed' in order to obfuscate a wider malaise in the government-appointed Railway Executive which had taken over the managerial responsibilities of the independent railway companies for the duration of the war – supposedly to improve cooperation between railway companies, and the smooth management of the many additional troop trains which the war effort required.

There is no doubt that signalman Meakin was initially in the wrong by forgetting to put the locking collar on the signal lever which would have kept the signals at danger. Had he done so, and notified the boxes further up and down the line, both the express train and the troop train might have been halted before they ever reached Quintinshill.

But Meakin was working well after the official end of his long overnight shift because his relief signalman, Tinsley, had not turned in for work. He lived about a mile away and usually walked to the signal-box but, on that morning, he had not arrived until well after his shift had officially started.

Tinsley apparently was in a confused state when he signed on duty, failing to carry out the routine tasks he had done at the start of every shift in his seven and a half years as a signalman. His claim that he simply forgot that the local train was standing outside his signal-box was considered unrealistic – he had, after all, arrived late for his shift having travelled on that very train, and could still see it out of the signal-box window. But his claim that he forgot may very well have been true as it seems highly likely that he was a long-time sufferer from epileptic fits – something which should have debarred him from ever becoming a signalman.

Indeed, when the decision was made to arrest him on the day of the disaster, his doctor had written a letter seeking a temporary postponement of the arrest as he was suffering an epileptic fit at the time.

Did the CR know of his medical condition? If so, how had he been passed fit to become a signalman in the first place? Why was his medical condition never raised as an issue in the Board of Trade enquiry?

Little remained of the burned-out sleeping car on the northbound express except the main underframe and a few upright struts. The delay in getting to the scene, and the lack of sufficient water meant that over three hours had passed before the Carlisle firemen could actually get to work.

THE RAILWAY DISASTER NEAR CARLISLE.
ALL THAT REMAINED OF THE SLEEPING CAR.

above: One of the mass funerals for the military dead. Even during a war, soldiers were assigned to line the streets of Leith as the corteges slowly trundled past. There was something especially poignant about so many dying on home soil, without ever taking part in the war they had been training for. They were buried with full military honours, at Rosebank Cemetery, each coffin draped in the Union Flag. Few of their colleagues who fell in France would be given such an honour.

left: The message from 'Jim' on the back of the funeral card tells 'Maud' of his 'heavy battery' leaving for France. He possibly wrote to Maud in late May or early June 1915, and anticipated being in France by late June, placing him on the Western Front in the middle of the battle for Festubert where Britain suffered 16,648 casualties. One wonders if he ever made it back home. Putting this sort of information on an open postcard would not have been tolerated by the censors, so 'Jim' must have sent it inside an envelope, paying a penny rather than a ha'penny to do so.

FUNERAL OF 100 VICTIMS OF THE GRETNA GREEN RAILWAY DISASTER AT LEITH WITH MILITARY HONOURS.
The long line of transport waggons containing the coffins passing through the town to the cemetery.

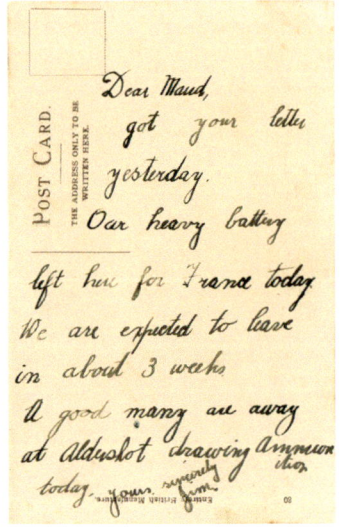

When Tinsley came to give evidence to the enquiry, he described an 'agreement' between himself and Meakin to break the rules. That contradicted Meakin's evidence and caused much consternation.

'I am 32 years of age and have been over 8 years in the service – as signalman for $7^1/_2$ years, and for the last $5^1/_2$ years signalman in Quintinshill Box. On the morning of Saturday, 22nd May, I came on duty at 6.32 a.m., but signed the register book as taking duty at 6 a.m. This had been the practice at Quintinshill between my mate and myself to avoid getting up so early in the morning. This was done without the knowledge of the District Inspector or of the District Superintendent, and to keep our action from their knowledge the night signalman kept a note in pencil of the train signals from 6 a.m. until the change in shift was made at 6.30 a.m., and the day shift signalman entered the times in the train register book after signing his name and recording the time as 6 a.m.'

Both Tinsley and Meakin, and fireman Hutchinson were indicted at the Coroner's Court in Carlisle – an odd decision as the disaster took place in Scotland which had, and still has, its own separate legal system. They were subsequently charged with gross negligence and culpable homicide in Scotland, and put on trial in Dumfries. Hutchinson was found not guilty, but for Meakin and Tinsley, the verdict was guilty, with 18 months' and three years' imprisonment respectively.

Suggestion that the handling of the case was a conspiracy to protect the Caledonian Railway and the Railway Executive and scapegoat the signalmen were fuelled by the fact that the families of the two men were taken care of financially by the railway company while they were in prison, and both men were given jobs on their release from prison – although not as signalmen.

There were many other accidents during 1915 – a remarkable number of them due to signalling errors – but they were all overshadowed by the horror of Quintinshill.

The first of the year had been the collision at Ilford Junction (*see below*) where 10 died and at least 500 were injured to varying degrees, followed by another collision at Smithy Bridge on the L&YR when a signal was, again, passed at danger.

The Weedon disaster on the L&NWR in which 10 died and 64 were injured on 14 August was attributed, unusually, to poor maintenance of the locomotive, and the year ended with the accident on 17 December on the NER which left 19 dead and 82 injured at St. Bede's near Jarrow. That one was blamed on multiple causes, including driver error, signalman's error, failure to carry out the requirements of Rule 55 – yet again – and inadequate signalling arrangements with gas lighting in the coaches once again cited amongst the secondary causes.

Despite the appalling loss of life over the preceding fifteen years, lessons, it seems, took a surprisingly long time to be learned.

In any other year, the first fatal accident of 1915, which occurred on New Year's Day, at Ilford Station, might have been expected to be the year's worse – with 10 killed and more than 500 injured. The crash was deemed to have been caused by a combination of driver error – passing a signal at danger – and excessive speed. The Clacton to London express running at about 50mph ran into the 8.20am local train from Gidea Park to Liverpool Street, running at about 15 mph.

INDEX

9th Avenue 'L' disaster 1905 12

Abergele disaster 1868, memorial 8
Amberswood Junction disaster, Wigan 1900 21-2
Andover crash, 1914 102
Aspinall, John 31
Aylesbury disaster 1904 37-8

Barnsley Photo Company 44-5, 47
Batchelder Brothers, photographers 80-82, 84
Beardmore, William & Company 97
Blairgowrie Station, 1906 2, 51-3
Blundellsands disaster 1905 39-41, 43, 45, 77, 88
Board of Trade, the 9, 20-22, 25-7, 43, 58-9, 65, 72-4, 78-9, 88-9, 101, 104-9
Bouch, Thomas 19
Bridgeport, Connecticut disaster 15
Brightwell, Leonard 9
Broughton-in-Furness Station 5, 7

Caledonian Railway (CR) 2, 24, 51, 107-9
California State Fair 10
'Carbic' acetylene lights 85-6
Carr Bridge disaster, 1914 103
Carter, Charlotte Mary 83
Charing Cross Station, Glasgow 27
Cherbourg disaster 1910 14
Churchward, George Jackson 35, 37
Colchester disaster, 1913 96-9
Contich disaster 1908, Belgium 13
Coventry Albany Road derailment, 1904 34-5
Cowans Sheldon cranes 56, 86
Creswell, George 66
Crippen & Company, Wigan and Pemberton 21
Cromer Express disaster, 1905 47-9
Crush, Texas 10
Crush, William 13
Cudworth disaster 1905 44-7
Cullingworth & Company, photographers 97

Daily Mirror, The 87
Dean, William 63, 68
Deane, Jarvis 'Joe' 14
Dick, Kerr & Company 41
Dickens, Charles 7
Ditton Junction disaster, 1912 92-5
Druitt, Lieutenant-Colonel Edward 43, 95
Drummond, Dugald 55

Duyshart, Alida, photographer 47
Duyshart, Pieter Johannes, photographer 47

Ebbw Junction collision, 1907 63
Edward VII, King 79
Elliot Junction disaster, 1906 62
Empson, Ellis Vernon, photographer 29

Felling disaster, 1907 70
'Flying Welshman' accident 1904 35-7
Ford, Philip T., photographer, Widnes 94,
Friedland Station derailment, 1909 75-6
Furness Railway (FR) 5, 7, 31
Futcher, F., photographer 54

Gale & Polden, postcard publishers 71
Glasgow & South Western Railway (G&SWR) 2, 24, 26, 31, 59
Glasgow St. Enoch's Station disaster 1903 31
Gothard, Warner, of Barnsley 44-7, 72, 75-8, 82, 96, 100-101
Grantham disaster, 1906 55-7
Great Eastern Railway (GER) 25-6, 47-8, 96-7
Great Central Railway (GCR) 37-8, 73, 90-92
Great Northern Railway (GNR) 55
Great Western Railway (GWR) 35-7, 63, 65, 68, 79
Gretna Station derailment 1901 23-4, 26

Hackney Downs station 25
Hall Road disaster, Blundellsands 1905 39-41, 43, 45, 77, 88
Hartley Brothers, photographers 28
Hastings, G., photographer 70
Hebden Bridge disaster, 1912 95
Helsby, James Barrow, photographer 83-4
Highbridge derailment, 1909 79
Highland Railway (HR) 103
Holden, James 68
Hopkinstown disaster, 1911 89-90
Horwich Locomotive Works 31
Huddersfield disaster, 1905 42, 48
Hull, Old Paragon Station 49
Huskisson, William 5-6

Ilford Junction collision, 1915 111
Illustrated London News, The 27, 64-5, 81, 86-7
Illustrations Bureau, The 86
Irving, George Washington, photographer 90
Isthmium Canal Company 12

King Edward VII 79

INDEX

Kirtlebridge disaster 1906 58
Kontich disaster 1908, Belgium 13

Lancashire & Yorkshire Railway (L&YR) 21, 26, 29, 31, 39-42, 77, 91-2, 95
Lankester & Company, photographers 48
Lawless, Ellen 7
Leven Viaduct disaster 1903 32-3
Le Neve-Foster, Annie 74
Lewis, Jack, photographer Swansea 36
Linstead, J. 25
Liverpool & Manchester Railway (L&MR) 1-2
Liverpool Overhead Railway 74
Liverpool, Waterloo Station disaster 1903 28-31
Llanelli disaster 1904 35-7
Lloyd George, David 65
London, Brighton & South Coast Railway (LB&SCR) 80, 86-7
London & Manchester Railway (L&MR) 67
London & North Eastern Railway (LNER) 100
London & North Western Railway 26, 33, 42, 48-9, 64-5, 75, 87-8, 92-4, 111
London & South Western Railway 22, 55,71

Meredith, Mary, poet 66
Messer, Horace Charles, photographer 54
Metropolitan Railway 71
Midland Railway (MR) 45, 78
Miraflores, Panama, bridge collapse, 1910 12
Monair, D. G., photographer 51-2
Morter, Ernest, photographer 99
Museum of Tsar Alexander III St. Petersburg 11

National Railway Museum, York 21, 31
Newport, Monmouthshire, accident, 1907 68
New York City, 9th Avenue 'L' disaster 12
North British Railway (NBR) 77, 100-101
North Eastern Railway (NER) 20, 26, 45, 59, 59, 111

Observer, The 82-3
Odessa, Minnesota disaster 1911 11

Pall Mall Gazette, The 71
Panama Canal 12
Parkside Station 5
Penrith Station wreck 1903 32-3
Perceval, Spencer, photographer 78
Pontypridd disaster, 1911 89-90
Pringle, Major J. W. 27, 78, 101-03

Quintinshill disaster, 1915 104-111

Rainhill Trials 4-5
Reading disaster, 1914 102
Reuters News Agency 85
Robinson, John G. 73
'Ruby Reflex' camera 87

Rule 220 33
Rule 55 98-9, 106-8, 111

St. Bede's, Jarrow, disaster 1915 111
St. Helens Junction 1
Salisbury Boat Train disaster 1906 53-55
Saltcoats Station 2-3
Sharnbrook disaster, 1909 76-7
Shrewsbury disaster, 1907 64-7
Sketch, The 81, 87
Slough Station collision, 1900 20
South East & Chatham Railway (SE&CR) 78
Spalding, Fred Jnr., photographer 47, 49
Sphere, The 87, 90
SS *City of New York* 55
Staplehurst disaster 1865 7
Stephenson, Robert 5
Stoat's Nest disaster, 1910 80-

Tassell, Frederick William, photographer 58
Taunton collision, 1907 67-8
Tay Bridge disaster, 1879 16-19, 56
Times, The 85
Thingley Junction accident, 1907 63
Thornton Pickard camera 87
Tonbridge Junction collision, 1909 78-9
Topical Press Agency 80-81, 83-4, 93
Tunbridge Wells derailment 1905 49-50
Twickenham 22

Ulleskelf disaster, 1906 59-60

Valentine, James & Son 19
von Donop, Lieutenant-Colonel 22, 91, 99
Virginia Water 22

Waterloo Station disaster 1903, Liverpool 28-31
Wakesfield, ~Charles Cheers 85
Waleswood collision 1907 69
Warner Gothard of Barnsley 44-7, 72, 75-8, 82, 96, 100-102
Webb, Francis 75
Webb, Mary, poet 66
Weedon disaster, 1915 111
Wellingborough disaster 1898 9, 18
Wellington, Duke of 5
Westerley, Rhode Island derailment, 1911 15
Whale, George 64-5
Wigan North Western Station 6
Winchburgh disaster 1872 8
Witham Station disaster, 1905 47-89
Wombwell disaster, 1911 90-92
Woodhouse Junction disaster, 1908 72-3
Wright, Fred, photographer and publisher 102

Yorke, Lieutenant-Colonel H. A. 9, 88